Three Women and the Men They Dance With

Written by
T. L. Messner

PublishAmerica
Baltimore

First printing

ISBN: 1-60703-953-2 (softcover)
ISBN: 978-1-4489-1653-5 (hardcover)
PUBLISHED BY PUBLISHAMERICA, LLLP
www.publishamerica.com
Baltimore

Printed in the United States of America

*This book is dedicated to my three children.
They are the light in my soul and the breath of my life!
I am so proud of all of you!! It is a joy to see the wonderful, loving
Parents you have all become!*

Anyone that has lived for any length of time can tell you that that they have been several different people throughout their lives. The people in our lives, whether by choice or by birth, determine who we are at any given time.

This is the story of the three very different women I have been throughout my life and the trials or dances that I had to learn along the way.

The first woman was: LOST AND LONELY.

The second woman was: SCARED AND WORTHLESS.

And the third woman is: LOVING LIFE AND LIVING HER DREAMS.

As we go through this life, the trials and triumphs we experience become the dances we learn. These dances will shape us into the person we ultimately become. We learn that some dances are easy, while others will try us to our very souls. We will stumble, and we will fall, but the most important thing to learn is that all the steps are necessary to take us back to our home in Heaven.

Others in my life may have perceived these events differently, there are two sides to every story after all, but this is my life... as seen through my eyes.

Some of the names have been changed for the protection of the innocent people that had their lives blended into mine. Also, the names of the men in my life have been changed, because even though they were very hurtful to me, I would never want to cause hurt to anyone else.

Three Women
and the Men
They Dance With

Chapter One

I was born in 1957. I was the second of four girls born to my parents, George and Sylvia.

The home my parents made was a good Christian home! My parents attended church regularly and they both had a great love for God and our Savior Jesus Christ. Their home was filled with love and joy.

My dad sang barbershop all the years we were growing up. Barbershop music is created when a group of men or women get together and harmonize songs. Our house was filled with music that was written years before my birth. I felt like the blending of their voices was as magical as angels singing from Heaven. I loved to listen with my eyes closed and picture the angels singing to me. I never doubted that Dad loved God and he had great faith in Him.

Dad didn't very often share his feelings with me, but I could see by his actions that he tried his best to be a good Christian and follow the teachings of God. He made sure that we were taught the teachings of Christ in our home and we strived to live by those teachings.

I don't remember Dad being home very often; the majority of

his time was spent at his practices and performances. Most of our family vacations were centered around his shows.

Our family would spend days crammed into the station wagon driving to Dad's next show. We went to campgrounds and slept in tents most of the time, but these became adventures that I loved. I had a great time getting to know the families of the other singers in Dad's quartet and loved to see the excitement shared by the whole group when Dad's quartet would win the competition.

My whole family enjoyed meeting the members of different quartets from all over the United States at these shows. Dad's quartet, "The Brine Shrimp Four," won many trophies throughout the years I was growing up. He was born to be a performer and Dad shined when he was on the stage. The songs he would sing made me feel like I was stepping back into another time when the world was a very different place.

Dad's family was of German descent. He had dark hair (what there was of it) and hazel eyes. As long as I can remember he had the comb-over because of a thinning hairline. He wasn't very tall, about five feet seven inches, but Dad was handsome!

Mom was very lovely! She liked to be called Sue instead of Sylvia. Her family was a mixture of Irish and English descent. She had naturally curly red hair and lovely brown eyes that sparkled all the time. Mom was only about five feet two inches tall but she never seemed small to me.

Mom's birth mother died just days after giving birth to her but she was adopted by her older sister Grace so that she could stay with the family. Even though Grace was a newlywed and just starting her life with Irvan she agreed to take Mom into her home to raise her as her own child.

The doctor didn't expect my mom to live because she was so small and malnourished; however, with the love and care she was given by her sister Grace she thrived. Her survival was amazing to the doctors. Mom used to tell us that Grandma Grace took her home from the hospital in a shoe box wrapped in cotton. She told us that incubators were not available for babies in her small town so this was the best way doctors could keep the babies warm.

Mom also loved to sing, but she did most of her singing at church. She also loved everything crafty. She could turn an egg carton into a work of art. She always had some craft project in the works in our house and our home was filled with her creations.

Mom loved nature and animals and could find beauty in anything. I remember many times stopping the car on the freeway for Mom to pick some interesting plant she had seen while driving by. On one occasion, Mom stopped to pick some weeds she had seen; I didn't know what they were but they were beautiful. About ten minutes after driving off, the car filled with bees. Mom brought the car to a screeching halt and we all ran screaming. We laughed so hard that it brought tears to our eyes. After that she made sure to shake the plants well before bringing them into the car.

Mom also loved genealogy. She spent hours researching our relatives, and she had massive books filled with the history of our family. She loved to take us to old cemeteries and read the names on the headstones. She would then go home and look through her books to see if they were related to us.

Mom had a great faith in God and our Savior Jesus Christ and was open in sharing her faith with us girls. She shined by her example and strength in God.

Penny was the firstborn daughter. She was the first child and first grandchild on both sides of the family. Penny had long dark hair and deep brown eyes and the beautiful features of my dad's side of the family. She was adored by everyone. She was the apple of Dad's eye, Daddy's little princess, and she knew it. She fit into the role of firstborn very nicely.

When I was born two years later, my father was sure that he would get the son he always wanted. Mom and Dad had decided that my name would be Terri regardless of the outcome. When I turned out to be a girl, they added the middle name of Lou so that my name would rhyme with Penny's. Her name is Penny Sue. This made my name a little more feminine.

I was born bald, but it was soon apparent that my hair would be red like Mom's. And as it grew it was also curly like Mom's. I also had brown eyes, but mine weren't as bright as Penny's; mine were a darker brown, almost black.

What I didn't know as a child was that Mom hated her red curly hair and therefore never wanted a child with red curly hair. The effects of these two physical attributes, first not being a boy and second having curly red hair, would become apparent as the years went by. It felt like I was starting my life with two strikes against me. Mom would get frustrated with my curly hair and instead of trying to find a cute style for the curls, she would simply cut it short. I always felt like a boy with my butchered hair.

Sheri was born one and a half years after me. Sheri was "The Pretty One." With long blonde hair and golden brown eyes she shined for the entire world. She seemed to be everyone's favorite. People seemed to flock to Sheri; they all wanted to hold and cuddle her when she was young, and she loved it. She loved having her picture taken, and the camera loved her. She always looked beautiful and stole the show wherever we went.

My youngest sister Peggy was the baby. Peggy was three years younger than me. She was named after my dad's mother, Margaret. She also had red hair; however, hers was long and flowing and beautiful. Peggy was also very lovely. She had golden brown eyes and beautiful olive skin.

Peggy had some medical problems as a young girl, and she was actually one of the first children to ever undergo plastic surgery.

I don't remember exactly how old she was at the time, but I think she was around five. The surgery was nothing life threatening, but it was something new to our family. The procedures at the time required a lot of healing time, and extensive bandage changes. The skin used for the replacement skin was kept attached to the body until the grafting was completed. Peggy's arm was attached to her stomach for months.

Her recovery required a great deal of attention, so Peggy was spoiled by everyone. We were all careful not to let her get bumped or hurt. I felt like she was very fragile and I became very protective of her. I always tried to help her whenever I could.

As I was growing up I wasn't considered beautiful, and I felt my parents were disappointed because I wasn't the boy they both wanted. I felt like I was "just there." I didn't fit in. I never caused any trouble and was always smiling. I was the "good girl," and I was content to just blend in. As a result, I never felt "special" to anyone.

We grew up going to church every Sunday. I heard all the lessons and learned all the songs about how Jesus loves us. I thought I knew what they meant. I tried to always be good so God would love me.

The state that I grew up in was one that allowed prayer in all of its academic activities. Before school activities we would pray, and meals were always started with a prayer of thanks. I knew that God existed, I just never felt different from anyone else in his eyes.

I wanted to be someone "SPECIAL" in my family, but I wasn't. At home in this family of beautiful people, I felt like the ugly duckling!

As we grew older, Mom would bring home stray people the way others would bring in stray animals. Not to say that the animals weren't also taken in. She couldn't see allowing anyone or anything to be left without a place to be safe and loved.

This was a great Christian thing to do; however, it made me feel even more left out because I thought these strangers were more important to her than I was. And I was her daughter!

During my childhood we moved a lot, one time just across the street. I never questioned why we moved so much, but I did learn to make each move a new adventure. I knew that if I was going to have any friends I had to learn how to reach out and make new ones each time we moved.

My sisters would send me over to the neighbors' houses to find out if there were any children living there. It was my job to make friends with them and bring them home for everyone else to meet. Most of the time they would become my sisters' friends and leave me with no one again.

I attended six different elementary schools, three different junior high schools, which were seventh, eighth and ninth grades. I attended the same high school for all three years, but during those years I lived in three different houses. I was able to create some great friendships during the years I was growing up, but they never lasted very long. Sadly I can't remember more than a handful of their names.

I really wanted one lifelong friend that would be by my side for my whole life, but I never found one. So still I didn't feel "special" to anyone!

As I grew up I was a tomboy, as close to a boy as I could get for my dad. I loved being outside climbing trees and swinging from their branches. We would play outside all day long and only went in the house when it got dark because that was the rule. We could have stayed out all night if it was allowed. Once in a while we were allowed to play hide-and-seek in the dark. My sisters and I never ran out of ways to have fun. We would play kickball in the streets and we had big metal roller skates that attached to the bottom of our shoes. We wore the roller skate keys around our necks like jewelry. The year that clackers were sold in the stores my mom learned how to make them herself and we had a great time bruising up our arms by swinging them and making a great amount of noise. We made our own hop-scotch frames out of chalk on the driveway and spent hours playing board games such as Battleship and Monopoly.

We would put together spook alleys at Halloween time and we loved getting homemade popcorn balls and cookies when we went trick-or-treating. It wasn't until I was a teenager that people started putting razor blades into apples and doing horrible things to others simply for the joy of hurting someone else. The world we lived in was a safe place during my childhood. We would occasionally hear of something bad happening to someone, but it never affected us personally, so to us our world was safe and fun.

When we went camping and fishing as a family, I learned to bait my own hooks with disgusting worms, just so I could impress Dad. I found that I enjoyed the solitude of sitting by the lake with the fishing pole in my hand listening to the sounds of the world. With the ever-present influence of music in my life, I learned to love singing. I was always singing or humming wherever I went. These were usually made-up songs because they made me happy. Dad would remind me that if I wasn't quiet the fish would be scared away, so I learned to keep singing my songs in my head.

I enjoyed watching my sisters get all upset when they had to touch the worms. They would screech and get all girly and refuse to bait their hooks, so I would do it for them. Dad would get very excited when we caught a fish. I didn't like eating the fish, but I enjoyed catching them.

At home my sisters and I would hang blankets on the clothesline to use as a curtain for the talent shows that we would perform. Mom would watch our shows once in a while if she had time, but she was extremely busy with her craft projects or canning fruits and making candy. She won numerous ribbons at the state fairs for her candy. Our performances were usually for our own enjoyment, and more than anything I would sing a song. I was sure that I would be a great singer someday. Though Dad's life was centered on singing I can't remember him ever wanting to watch me perform at our homemade shows. I wanted him to be proud of me and encourage me to sing, but I felt that the only music he was interested in was his own.

I remember at Christmastime my father would put the stereo speakers in the front windows of our house and blast Christmas music out into the neighborhood. I can't remember anyone ever complaining. I knew all the songs and could be heard singing all the way down the block.

Speaking of Christmas, it became a bittersweet holiday for me. My birthday is December 20; as if being so close to Christmas wasn't bad enough, Penny's was December 22, and Peggy's was Christmas Day. I never had a birthday party just for me. We had family parties for all three of us, usually on Penny's birthday because it was in the middle. All my presents were marked Happy Birthday and Merry Christmas all on one gift.

I never got to have a party at school because we were always out for the holiday. Again this made me feel as if I was left out and unimportant. I'm sure Penny and Peggy felt the same way, but we never talked about it. We never seemed to talk about anything that involved feelings.

When I was about nine, Dad asked me to go golfing with him. I was very excited because he hadn't asked any of my other sisters to go. I thought that I was going to get to spend the day with Dad learning to play golf so we could play together. I found out when we got there that Dad brought me along because I was good at finding things. He sent me off into the trees to find golf balls that had been abandoned by other golfers. We went home with a large bag full of golf balls, but my dream of doing something special with Dad was shattered. Dad took me several more times, but always with the intention of finding golf balls. I never got a chance to learn how to play the game. I again felt like I didn't matter as a daughter because Dad hadn't taken me to show off his wonderful daughter; I was just another person that could perform a function that was needed.

When I was about twelve, Mom decided that she wanted to learn to ski. She told us that she could only afford for three of us to take the lessons. Penny didn't have time for us and didn't want to go. I really wanted to, but I knew that Sheri and Peggy would have their feelings hurt if they weren't able to go, so I told Mom that I didn't really want to and told her to take Sheri and Peggy. It wasn't until Sheri broke her thumb doing cartwheels in the snow that I was able to go with Mom and Peggy. There were only two lessons left and I was so far behind the students my age that I had to stay on the bunny slopes with the little children. I only went skiing a few times after that because I never felt like I learned enough to not embarrass myself. I would watch everyone else fly down the mountain with such ease and beauty and I only knew how to snow plow. Even then I looked awkward and ungraceful so I just didn't go anymore.

Growing up we didn't have very much in the way of material things. We shopped at discount stores and had a lot of hand-me-downs, but I never complained. We didn't have all the things that we wanted, but we always had everything that we needed. My sisters and I were content in our world.

Mom made most of our dresses growing up. We had all the really cute matching dresses and looked like the perfect little family. We always spent Sundays going to church and doing things as a family. This was the one night that everyone was together for dinner. Mom always made a special meal on Sundays. Though I felt like an outsider in my family, our home was always filled with love. It was a comfortable place to live, and I enjoyed bringing my friends home with me where they always felt welcome.

As we grew older Penny became part of the adult world early and left the rest of us behind. She had a job and a boyfriend and didn't have time for her sisters anymore. She and Mom argued a lot, though I didn't know what about; it just seemed that they were always angry at each other. I tried not to get into the middle of whatever the problem was because I didn't want either of them getting mad at me. I learned to mind my own business and not get myself into trouble. Dad helped Penny get a car when she was in high school, and she would drive us around occasionally, but that was the only time Penny and I spent together. She didn't include me in her grown-up world, and her life became very mysterious to me. She had become everything that I was led to believe we were supposed to become. She was a beautiful young woman with a boyfriend that adored her and a car that allowed her freedom.

Sheri became Mom's shadow and followed her around everywhere she went. She and Mom would ride our horses in parades, which for Sheri meant getting all the cool riding outfits and the glory of being seen by all the world. She never seemed to stop shining.

Sheri was happy being the "Special One." She was the only one that didn't have a birthday in December; hers was in July, which meant that she got all the cool parties and great gifts. I have to admit that I was jealous of Sheri and the special attention she always seemed to get from Mom.

I tried getting involved with the things Mom liked, but I had allergies and couldn't be around the horses. And when I tried helping with the gardening, I was given the job of pulling weeds. I got tired of the never-ending battle with weeds and soon gave up, leaving me to find other ways to gain Mom's approval. I never seemed to find the one thing that would make me stand out above the others.

Peggy liked getting us in trouble for not letting her join us in whatever we were doing. It wasn't that we didn't want her with us, but we wanted to be cool teenagers and we still thought of her as our baby sister. Peggy took dance lessons and was very creative with dancing. She would come home and teach us what she had learned and then we created our own routines. She had beautiful costumes for her performances which Mom helped make. Mom would make all the outfits for the dance club in exchange for Peggy's lessons.

Mom was also very active with our family reunions. She loved meeting with all the distant relatives and hearing family stories. I think she felt a need to connect with her real brothers and sisters. She was trying to find her own place in our world. Having been adopted she told us that she felt separated from her real family and wanted to fill the emptiness she felt inside. I had a lot of fun at these reunions, but I also felt lost in this sea of people that didn't notice me. As with all functions Sheri was the one that was always running off with our cousins, leaving Peggy and me to entertain the little children. Despite that fact that my family was always there, I just didn't feel like I belonged with them. I can't say that I never felt loved, I just never felt "special."

As with all children, each of us will remember the events of our lives differently. My sisters would probably tell an entirely different story, but this is the way I felt in my world at that time. I felt like part of a very happy family that I really didn't fit into.

Chapter Two

I was a good student and loved to learn. I got good grades and tried to find ways to get extra attention from my teachers. Because we moved so often, none of the teachers was in my life for very long, but being recognized for a short amount of time was better than not being noticed at all.

Throughout my life it seemed the kids that were the most tormented by everyone else flocked to me. They needed someone to be kind to them, and I was the one to do it. As great as it was being the one person they could reach out to, it made it difficult to fit in with the cool kids. And as I became a young woman being cool became even more important to me. I continued to be kind to them but tried to do it so that nobody would notice.

With all the moving around we did, I wanted to fit in as soon as possible. I knew that my time would be limited and I couldn't waste any of it working my way into the popular groups. So I smiled and said hello to everyone until one or two people would reach out to welcome me into their group of friends.

I tried to be as kind to everyone as I could while also being popular. I gave the appearance that I was confident and strong.

However, inside I felt like I was still struggling to be someone special.

In the ninth grade I received my first kiss from a boy!

Our church was doing a road show; it was like a talent show that traveled around to all the other church buildings in our area. And of course being the star that I thought I was, I wanted to be in it. That year Penny was asked to write the show. I only remember that it had a carnival theme. Penny chose me to sing the first solo part. It was only a few lines, but I'm sure that I did it as well as any real "star." My part was small, but I was performing and I loved it.

It was while doing this show that I first met Daniel. He was tall for a ninth grader; he was at least six feet tall. He had dark hair and dark eyes. His smile melted my heart. The phrase of "tall, dark and handsome" came to mind when I thought about him. It was scary for me to be noticed by a real boy, but it was also exciting. After performing the show four times, Daniel walked me home. It was in front of my house that night that I received my first real kiss. I was very nervous and excited, but the kiss ended quickly when Sheri came running out of the house to tease me.

Daniel and I stayed good friends for the next few months, but I soon learned that we were moving again and it broke my heart. Neither one of us was old enough to drive, so staying good friends didn't last very long. We tried to stay in touch, but phone calls didn't get made very often. And soon my first crush was crushed.

When I started high school the effects of feeling like I wasn't anyone special started to become more apparent to me.

Entering high school in a new area of town meant going into a school full of students that had been friends since the first grade. Groups had been already been established, and most of them were happy to stay with the group of friends they already had.

The freshman students had to share lockers with someone

else, which turned out to be a good thing for me. The first person I met was my locker mate Eva. We became good friends and Eva introduced me to her other friends. I soon felt like I was part of a group of my own.

As the year progressed I made many other friends. Launa moved into the school in the middle of my freshman year. I first saw her in choir class. She looked nervous so after class I approached her and I told her that I knew how it felt to be in a new school. I reached out to her and introduced her to everyone I knew. Launa lived in the same area I lived in so we were also able to spend time together away from school. My friend Karen, myself and Launa lived within three blocks of each other and the three of us became very close friends. We all got part-time jobs at the same fast food restaurant and spent a great deal of time together. This was the first time I felt like I belonged and was loved for who I was.

Throughout that year I made a lot of friends that were boys, but none of them thought of me as anything other than a friend. The boys would always come to me with their girlfriend problems. They never knew how hard it was for me to give them advice when I didn't know anything about being a girlfriend. I had never had any experience being one.

At the end of our freshman year the school had tryouts for the drill team. Launa, Karen and myself went to all the practices and spent our time away from school helping each other learn the routines we would have to perform for the tryouts. I was the only one of the three that was chosen to be in the Minerettes. I was thrilled but also sad because I wanted Launa and Karen to be there with me. I was afraid that our friendship would be hurt by the fact that I had been chosen and they weren't. They taught me that true friends don't let these things ruin their friendships, and they both continued to support me and nothing changed between us. They attended the sporting events and not only cheered for the teams but also for me. They were a blessing to my life.

I also started gymnastic classes and felt like I had finally found something I was good at. I was able to compete in several tournaments and had a way to show everyone that I did have a talent that made me stand out.

I had only two dates in the entire three years of high school. The first date was a dance I invited Tom to.

I first met Tom in the library at school. We started visiting almost every day. I would go looking for him on our lunch break, and he always seemed happy to see me. I thought for sure I was being very charming and would soon win his heart. Tom had blond hair and beautiful blue eyes. I felt like we were becoming good friends, so toward the end of that year I got up the nerve to invite him to a dance we were having for the drill team. He said yes and I was in Heaven.

The day before the dance Tom was out inner-tubing in the snow with his church group where he cut his behind on a large rock that he crashed into; he ended up with several stitches in his backside. Tom called to tell me that he would still go to the dance with me but he probably wouldn't be able to dance. That was alright with me because this was my first real date and I wasn't going to let anything get in the way. We attended the dance together with his seat donut in tow, but we left early because it was obvious that he was in pain.

That night I received my second "real kiss." After Tom told me that I was the first girl he had kissed since the first grade, I thought I had my first real boyfriend. I was floating on the clouds. Finally I was someone special.

Tom and I continued to go out with groups of friends, and I thought we were becoming close. We didn't really date, but I thought that would come in time. After all, Tom was spending time with me, even if there were a dozen other people with us.

It wasn't until the next school year when the first school dance arrived that I was made aware of my mistake. I was sure that Tom would invite me to go with him, but he didn't. I found out that he had invited a sophomore girl from his church instead. Tom told me that he had wanted to date this other girl for a long time but never had the nerve ask her out. He told me that going out with me gave him the courage to ask her out.

My dreams were shattered. I was heartbroken, but I couldn't let anyone else know it. I continued to put on a happy face and pretend that it didn't bother me. I still walked down the halls smiling and saying hello to everyone, but nobody knew how lonely I felt inside.

Date number two was my senior year. I received an invitation to the junior prom from a sophomore boy I barely knew. I think he must have been in one of my classes, but I can't say for sure which one. He just showed up by my locker one day and asked me to join him. I was so thrilled that someone asked me to the prom that I accepted his invitation. When we arrived at the dance I saw Tom there with his date. It was very painful to watch them dance and have fun. I felt like it should have been me dancing with Tom.

I think the young man that I was with must have asked me out on a dare. I don't remember talking to him again after the dance. And I can't even remember his name.

During my high school years I was none of the things that people considered "COOL." These were the days of long straight blonde hair and voluptuous figures (long before those things could be changed with plastic surgery) and beautiful model faces.

My hair, on the other hand, was naturally curly, and even worse, it was red. My mom continued to cut my hair very short because she told me that curly hair didn't look good long. Even in high school she wouldn't allow me to grow it longer than the top of my shoulders. And I have to admit that I didn't like my hair no matter what length it was. I just couldn't find a style that worked for me.

While my sisters were sporting their long beautiful hair, I learned to hate my curls. I tried my best in high school to tame the curls, but in the end it never resulted in that long sleek look. It was more like a full frizz, and if there was even the slightest hint of moisture in the air, all my efforts were in vain.

I was a gymnast and at five feet six inches and 98 pounds I had the figure of a two-by-four. I remember it became a great joke in my family to tease me about needing to put stockings into my bra. I never did it, but my sisters and even my dad would constantly tell me that I needed to.

It was during these years while watching all my friends dating and making the excuse that I had to work that I began to think there was something really wrong with me. Even my sisters had boyfriends. They were always going out while I stayed home or worked. I knew I was not a beauty queen, but I didn't think I was ugly either.

I was friendly and kind to everyone. So why wasn't I "special" to anyone?

My sisters and I never talked about our feelings with each other, and I was determined not to let anyone at school know that I was hurting, so these feelings just kept eating me up inside.

After graduation I was sure that Tom would figure out that I was really the one he wanted to be with, so I spent all my savings on a beautiful gold ID bracelet for him as a graduation gift. On the inside I had engraved "LOVE ALWAYS TERRI."

I delivered it to his house personally and I had dreams of him getting all emotional and telling me that he loved me too. However, I found out when I got to his home that he had another girl there with him. He barely looked at my gift and just said "Thanks." He then rushed me out the door.

I was totally humiliated!! Now I was certain there was something very wrong with me.

In the early '70s young women weren't encouraged to go out and make a career for themselves. We were encouraged to learn how to be good wives and mothers, so in order to do what was expected I took home economics classes and learned how to cook and sew. I was doing everything necessary to be the perfect wife, but I had to be realistic. There didn't seem to be any prospects for me in having a husband ,so I had to learn a trade.

Since the only jobs available to women were secretarial, I took those classes also. The highlight of our learning was shorthand and typing, but the big upcoming future of the world was keypunch. Keypunch was like a typewriter; it would punch holes onto cardstock. The holes were made in a coded pattern which would tell the computer what you wanted it to do. The cards were then fed into massive computers which read the punches and would run the programs. These were the first days of computers and it was very exciting.

I decided to attend a college about two hours away from home. I was living in the dorms with my great friends from high school, Launa and Karen, and three other girls we met when we arrived. It was fun because I fit into this little family group. We had great adventures together and spent time together as real families did. These girls became like sisters to me.

My mom was very excited for me because I was the first member of the family to attend college. I signed up to learn the great technique of keypunch for my future and had also decided that I would like to be a gymnastic teacher. So I signed up for all the necessary classes and tried out for the drill team. I was chosen to be a Thunderette. I was one of only nine girls chosen from over fifty contestants. This made me feel really great! We had beautiful costumes, and I felt like I had bloomed into a real girl. I felt like I finally was shining!

While I was in college I tried again to reconnect with Daniel, my first crush from junior high. While home for Christmas break I went to the house he was living in when I first met him. I was lucky to find him still living there. He told me that his family was going to move the next week.

He was as excited to see me again as I was to see him. We went out to dinner and a movie and while we were talking Daniel told me that he had joined the army. He said he would be leaving after Christmas. It just so happened that the day after Christmas my grandfather passed away and for whatever reason I totally lost my voice. I felt fine but I couldn't speak above a whisper. I couldn't call Daniel to tell him so I wasn't able to say goodbye to him before he left for the army.

We wrote letters to each other for several months. He would describe all the horrible things the war had done. It was the end of the Vietnam War, but there was still some fighting taking place.

Soon the letters stopped coming. I didn't really know why, so I prayed that it wasn't because he had been injured, or even worse, killed. Daniel's family had moved and I didn't know how to find them. It was very difficult not being able to find out what happened to him.

It was during this first year of college that I found out my parents were getting divorced. I can't remember them ever arguing, or even talking about things being bad so I couldn't understand what had caused things to get so out of control. Neither Mom nor Dad ever sat down to talk to me about any of it; the divorce just happened. Mom called me at school to tell me that they were getting divorced and that Dad had moved out.

Our family never talked about important things together; we

more or less just shared the fun things. The really serious stuff was uncomfortable to discuss so it was left unsaid. I had very little contact with my father after he left. I didn't even know where he had moved to. Dad never tried to spend any time with me, and it didn't seem like he wanted anything to do with any of us anymore. I don't know if it was because he felt guilty for leaving us, or if he just didn't care enough to talk to me. I know he kept in touch with Penny, but I didn't feel like I was included in any part of his life anymore.

Mom would never say what happened either; she just cried a lot and prayed that Dad would come back. She would have taken him back in a minute if he had wanted to return. With Sheri and Peggy still living at home life became a struggle for Mom. She had to work more and money was really tight. I don't think Dad helped her out financially.

I soon learned that all the checks my dad had written for my college classes had bounced so I had to leave school and get a job to pay back the money already spent.

I found a job at a local grocery store and worked long hours to pay off my debt. I tried to help Mom out by giving her some money for food, but I didn't have very much to give.

My friends were now making wedding plans and I hadn't even had a serious date. At the age of nineteen I thought I was going to be an old maid. All the things we were raised believing would fall into place as we became adults weren't happening to me. There was no knight in shining armor riding into my life to love and adore me. I couldn't even find that frog that needed kissing.

Later that year a young man I was working with at the grocery store started to tease me in a friendly way. He would flip rubber bands at me between customers to get my attention. When he asked me out on a date I felt like I was finally being noticed.

Mitch was six feet two inches tall and had a baby face. He had blond hair and blue eyes and was very cute. I could tell that he hadn't dated much because he seemed really shy around girls. We dated for a short time and started talking about getting married. After all, that was what we were supposed to do. I believed that I would never get another chance, so when he purposed I accepted.

Although I never felt that "TV" romance kind of love for Mitch, I was willing to take what I could get. I needed to show the world that someone wanted me. We didn't really know each other very well, but I decided that we could learn as time went on. Just before my twentieth birthday I married Mitch. We had a small ceremony in the clubhouse where Mitch's sister lived. I wore Penny's wedding dress, and because money was tight we kept the wedding small and simple.

Chapter Three

I didn't even know how to be a girlfriend, let alone a wife. Mitch and I lived more as roommates than husband and wife. I knew nothing about men. Having had no brothers, the only thing I remembered Mom ever saying was that there was nothing beautiful about a man's body. My sisters and I never talked about anything sexual. We weren't even comfortable talking about girl stuff. We never said aloud the words "sex," "periods," or anything else that was considered private. Any discussions about relationships were strictly avoided in our home.

Therefore I felt that anything to do with these private issues was meant to be secret.

Passion and affection were way beyond anything I had known. There wasn't really either of them in our marriage anyway. What I learned about relationships was on-the-job training.

Most of what I was learning was uncomfortable and awkward. I felt like I was playing house. I took on the duties of housekeeping and cooking, all the things I had learned in home ec. Mitch took over the role as man of the house. He paid all the bills and took charge of all the financing. Mitch would come home with some new idea for love making and the thought of it would turn my stomach. I could never let myself feel comfortable with intimacy. I felt like it was dirty. Because sex was a topic that was TABOO in our home growing up, it felt wrong to be doing these things. Even though I was married now, I still couldn't make myself enjoy it. So I just went along with whatever was expected of me so that I could be the good wife.

I turned over my paycheck to Mitch so that he could pay the bills, and I was given an allowance for lunches at work. Usually $2.00 a day, just enough for a nice salad and drink at the deli. I later learned that Mitch would take all the guys from the produce department where he was working out to lunch. They would take turns buying for everyone. I'm sure that the amounts he was spending were well over the $2.00 per day that I was receiving. But again as the peacekeeper, I never said anything to him about it.

After we were married I received a promotion at work and I was making good money, but Mitch never gave me any of it to spend on myself. He would give me a check for groceries once in a while, but if there was anything else I needed, he would go shopping with me and pay for everything. I was on a tight budget, and I just assumed that it was because it was taking all the money we made to pay the bills. I didn't feel that it was my place to ask any questions about the money because that was "the man's job." Again, I was focused on keeping everything peaceful and happy.

Mitch started getting angry about silly things such as too much bread in the meatloaf. He started yelling and throwing things. My time at home was spent trying to smooth things over and restore peace. I wanted to be the "perfect wife" but I felt like I was failing.

Mitch and I worked at the same grocery store, but we worked different shifts, so we weren't home together very often. That is why I was so shocked when I became pregnant the next year. It was as much a shock to Mitch as it was to me. We had never really talked about having a family and didn't quite know what to do. I can't say that it was an exciting time in our marriage, because I felt Mitch's frustration. He said he wasn't ready to be a father. I wasn't really ready to be a mother either, but I knew that I would do whatever I needed to for this baby.

As woman number one I didn't even feel like a woman, I felt more like a little girl playing house. I was lost and lonely and prayed for the strength to get through this hurdle and find a way to be a good mother.

I didn't know anything about being a mom. I wasn't even comfortable being myself. I felt lost in a woman's body, and I didn't have anyone to talk to about all this mother stuff. My sisters had gone on with their own lives, and we didn't see each other very often anymore. Penny had married the love of her life and now had a daughter. Sheri married her high school boyfriend, and Peggy was living at home with Mom. Mom was spending her days trying to find where she fit into this world of divorce that she had been thrown into. Even though my sisters and I had been very close while growing up, we didn't seem to need each other anymore after I got married.

Mitch and I went through these days not really knowing what to do. He never wanted to be part of anything involving the pregnancy or any of the plans for childbirth. I went to all the doctor's visits alone and did whatever I could to make sure that my baby would be healthy, while still getting by on just my $2.00 allowance for lunch. I worked full-time until the end of my pregnancy.

I can't remember even talking about the baby with Mitch until three weeks before my due date when I found out that I was having twins. Ultrasounds weren't done in those days unless the doctor thought there was something wrong. And since everything was going well, no testing had been done. At the appointment three weeks before my due date my doctor said that he thought he could hear two heartbeats, but it could just be an echo. After the ultrasound showed that there were indeed two babies I was really lost as to what to do next.

I was scared to tell Mitch that there would now be two babies instead of one. I didn't know how he would react. When I finally told him, he seemed to be indifferent about the news. My mom was the most excited. She said that she had always dreamed of having twins and thought that it would be so much fun. Mom and I hadn't spent very much time together since I left home, but with this news she tried to spend more time with me. She was the one that bought all the things I would need for my babies.

I prayed each night that I would be able to make my twins feel more special than I had felt my entire life. I knew that I would be on my own in teaching them about real love, but I wasn't sure that I knew real love myself.

Just before the delivery Mitch and I discussed possible names for the twins. Mitch was hoping that at least one of them would be a boy. This was the most we talked during the whole pregnancy. On the day before my due date Mom came to visit and Mitch and I went for a drive with her. After a few hours my labor started and we rushed to the hospital, one hour later my beautiful daughters were born.

On August 20 I gave birth to two marvelous daughters. Libby was six pounds four ounces and Rachell was five pounds ten ounces. They were both healthy; neither one of them needed to be in an incubator even though Rachell was a blue baby. Rachell was born breech, which meant she was born feet first. It turned out to be a good thing that they were healthy, because we found out that our insurance wouldn't cover any of their care until they were three months old.

As I sat in my hospital bed with my precious daughters in my arms I watched all the other mothers receive visitors and watched their husbands ooh and aah over their newborns. I wished that Mitch would feel the same way these other fathers felt, but he didn't.

The joy I felt the day my daughters were born was greater than I could have expected. I knew that they would become the most precious people I would ever have in my life and my life would be forever changed by being their mother.

I thought that when I brought these beautiful little blessings home from the hospital Mitch might feel differently about being their father. I found, however, that the hospital bills now became a reason for Mitch to be angry. He would get frustrated when the bills arrived, saying that he didn't know how he was going to pay them. Mitch seemed happy when he was with the girls, but I could sense his disappointment at not having a son.

He never took an active role in caring for the girls. It seemed as though Mitch avoided being home with us whenever possible. He never changed a diaper or bathed them. And because I was nursing them he didn't need to feed them either.

When my Grandma Grace came to help out I was relieved. It was great having her there to help me learn how to be a mother. I wouldn't have made it through those first few weeks without her help. She would rock one of the girls while I tried to nurse the other.

When Libby and Rachell were six weeks old Mitch told me that I needed to return to work because we needed the money. It was my responsibility to find childcare for the girls by myself. I tried my best to find a loving home for them while I had to be away. Several times I would find a loving woman to care for the twins, but they soon found out that it was more work than they had expected and they would back out of the deal. Thus leaving me hunting again for someone else.

I discovered that caring for twins was a great novelty for women to try, but not a reality for many to accomplish. My days off were usually spent trying to find another arrangement that would be permanent. If Mitch had a day off while I was working, he still had me take them to the babysitter; he never took care of the girls on his own.

I don't think Mitch intended to be cruel. He was just as lost about being a parent as I was, but at least I was trying to make it work. His approach to the situation was to withdraw and ignore what needed to be done. The frustrations we faced took their toll on our marriage; mistakes were made on both sides and hurts were caused, but we both knew that we weren't meant to be together. Our family just wasn't what it needed to be; we were far from a family.

The affection Mitch and I once had for each other could no longer be found, so when the girls were six months old Mitch and I were divorced.

I thought that I could start a new life as a new person. I really believed in second chances.

I felt even more lost and lonely now and still "nothing special" to anyone, but now I had two beautiful daughters depending on me to love and care for them.

With $75.00 a month for child support I had to work full-time to make ends meet. I have to admit I became a daycare mom. I trusted the majority of my motherly duties to other women. I loved my girls with all my heart, but I never felt like a good mom.

I had quit going to church after getting married and leaving home. The idea of returning crossed my mind from time to time, but after attending one meeting and having to try to keep two babies quiet for an hour I decided that it was too hard so I didn't make the effort again. I started to feel like God had given up on me and the things that were happening in my life were the things

I deserved for not being a better person. No one was missing me at church, so I felt like it didn't matter to anyone if I attended or not.

At the age of twenty-two I felt much older than my years. I was now labeled a divorcee. I felt that in order to fit into this world I now found myself a part of, I had to party and drink to be accepted. I knew that this party life was against everything I knew myself to be, and against everything that I had been taught growing up as the right way to live.

I was a lost soul desperate to find someone to validate me as a woman worth loving. I went places and did things that were horrifying to me, just for the sake of being part of something. I had never even tasted alcohol before and didn't know what I was supposed to do, but I was trying to find a way to feel good about myself. I admit that I went home with a few men I didn't know and never saw again, but being wanted for only one night was better than none at all. I still never enjoyed sex and felt even worse about it now because I knew that what I was doing was a sin. As each day went by I felt that God was more ashamed of me, and I didn't feel like I even deserved His love.

I became consumed by this feeling of loneliness and couldn't seem to find a way out. I wasn't sure where I needed to go in order to find the things that would bring happiness back into my life.

It was while out drinking one night that I met the man that would be my next husband. I don't really remember meeting him that night because I was drunk. He was actually flirting with the girl from work I had gone out with. We had gone out dragging State Street looking for guys and stopped to talk to a group of guys we passed. This other girl had given Jay my phone number because she didn't want her parents knowing that she was out looking for men.

It wasn't until Jay called my house looking for her that I knew what she had done. Jay and I started talking almost every night for several hours. He shared with me some of the details of his family and he would be joking around with his five-year-old niece while we were on the phone together. Jay sounded like a fun person to be around so we decided that we should meet face to face.

Chapter Four

When Jay came to my house I found him to be very handsome. He was five feet eight inches tall and had dark hair and hazel eyes. Because his father was half Native American Indian and his mother was Italian, Jay had beautiful olive skin that was beautifully tanned. We talked more that night and we both decided that we would like to spend more time together.

We started dating, and Jay was really kind to me and my girls. He would even take the girls to his house while I was working where he and his family took good care of them. Jay's niece Marie loved being around them. Libby and Rachell were one and Marie was five. They spent hours playing dolls, and they became very close.

I was still feeling the need to be loved so I fell for Jay very quickly. I didn't dare tell him about the horrible mistakes I had made, because I wanted him to love me. I couldn't take the chance that if he found out about the other men he would leave me. The fear of him finding out my secrets weighed heavy on my heart.

Jay and I were married six months later, and I admit that I didn't really know him very well, but I also knew that he didn't know me very well either. I just hoped that the past wouldn't matter.

We had a double wedding with Jay's older brother and his fiancée. The wedding was at the home of Jay's parents, James and Rosa. All my sisters and my dad were there for my wedding. It was great! Mom wasn't able to be there because she had moved to another state with her second husband, but I was glad to have most of my family with me. We had planned an outdoor wedding, so of course on the day of the wedding it rained. We moved everything inside, and it all turned out well despite the inconveniences.

Jay had been out of work, and his brother told him that he could get him a job at the wood-treating plant where he worked. This meant moving to another state ,so immediately after the wedding Jay and I moved away from my family and friends. By this time all of my sisters were married. Penny was married to the love of her life and had a daughter. Sheri had married her high school sweetheart and had a son, and Peggy had married a man I had only met one time, but I knew she was happy. Even though my relationship with them wasn't very close anymore, it was still hard leaving them 800 miles away.

I thought that moving to a new place would be an exciting new start for my life. I had always lived in the same state and wanted to see something new. I also felt like my secrets would be left behind and I would never have to take the chance of running into someone that might remember me and say something to Jay that would give away my secrets.

I thought that I would be able to forget all the bad things I had done and make myself into a new and better person. This was my opportunity to find out who I really was again without dwelling on my mistakes and failures as a woman and a mom.

I found out, however, shortly after we moved that the man I married was a Dr. Jekyll and Mr. Hyde.

Jay started getting angry and mean. It seemed that everything he had said that he loved about me, had now become things to be hated. I had always been a very friendly and kind person, I smiled and laughed a lot, but now Jay was telling me that I should be embarrassed to smile because he said my teeth looked like shit.

I knew that my smile wasn't the most beautiful in the world, but I had never before been told that I should be embarrassed to smile because of my teeth.

We were very seldom taken to the dentist as children, and I should have had braces but my parents couldn't afford them. My mom used to tell me to sit with my thumb pressed into my teeth and they would straighten out. I tried this technique for years, but needless to say, it never worked.

Because of Jay's comments I soon became embarrassed and didn't want to smile anymore. I started to see that he was right. I avoided letting anyone see my teeth and felt very self-conscious when I smiled.

Jay started telling me over and over that I was horrible and disgusting and that was why my first husband hadn't wanted anything to do with me. Soon I started to believe that maybe Jay was right. Jay did claim to love me after all, and maybe he was the only person that had the guts to tell me what my problems had been all along. No one else had wanted me, so I believed that what Jay was saying must be true!

Jay reminded me often that I was lucky that he wanted me despite all my horrible flaws because no one else would ever put up with me.

In a matter of a few months I was feeling even more awful about myself. I thought I finally knew why no one else could find me "special." I only wished that somebody would have told me sooner so that I wouldn't have gone on fooling myself into thinking that perhaps I could have been "special."

Jay's insults continued to wear away any self-esteem I had left, and I tried my best to blend into the background. I wore baggy old clothes and tried not to do anything that would draw attention from the outside world. I avoided leaving the house whenever possible.

When I finally realized that I was truly worthless, it was easy to just exist each day. My spirit was completely broken. There was absolutely no joy in our home, and I began regretting that my precious daughters were now doomed to this sad life I had brought them into. Knowing that I had done this to these sweet girls only made me more depressed, and I felt helpless to give them anything better.

I had come to believe that everything that was happening to me was my punishment for all the sins I had committed in the past, and I felt like I deserved everything that was happening to me. I thought that God had turned his back on me and had given up caring about what was happening in my life.

Without even realizing it woman number two was being transformed into a scared and worthless person with no hope of escaping the sadness that had entered my life. Nothing in my life thus far had prepared me to deal with the horrors that were unfolding. I had always been the peacemaker and had never learned to stand up for myself or even have to say "That is not okay!" This made me easy prey for the monster my husband was becoming.

My mom would occasionally call, but Jay would listen on the other line. He wanted to make sure that I didn't tell anyone about what was going on in our home. I was to play the part of a happy wife and make Mom believe that we were all happy and well. Jay would become very angry about everything I said during the conversation, so I was scared to death to say anything wrong. I knew that if I said anything he didn't like I would pay for it later. I think Mom could feel the tension through the phone, but she didn't know what to do about it. She felt that she was making trouble for me when she would call, so she quit calling as her way of protecting me. All my family lived in another state, so making calls to them was long distance. I knew if I called them the numbers would show up on the phone bills and Jay would see them and get angry, so I never dared to call them.

The letters I wrote were also read by Jay before they could be mailed; more of them were torn up and thrown away than were ever mailed, so I quit writing to my family and friends. Little by little he was smothering me and isolating me from everyone in my life. Jay had me in his prison and he had taken control of everything.

Jay would remind me that my family hadn't really cared about me anyway, so I shouldn't be so upset. I actually believed what he was saying because I thought if they did care about me they would be coming to rescue me from this horrible place.

My family didn't know how to protect me from Jay's anger, and they thought that by not getting involved they would keep me from getting into more trouble. As a family we had never had to deal with an abusive person before, so they didn't know what to do any more than I did. I never had the nerve to simply tell them what was happening, and I tried to make them believe that everything was fine.

The fact that I was now 800 miles away made it easier for Jay to accomplish his deceit and not let them see the truth of what my life had become. Jay was angry all the time, and I believed that it was my fault. I tried every day to be perfect and never say or do anything that would make him mad, but inevitably I would.

At first the abuse was verbal, but soon that wasn't enough for

Jay. When he couldn't make me cry by yelling at me or cutting me down about some physical attribute he started to hit me. Jay also started being cruel to Libby and Rachell.

He wasn't physically abusive to them at first, but he was always yelling at them for something they were doing, and then he would get angry at me for allowing them to make him mad. I wanted so much for my daughters to be happy and have a home filled with love and kindness, but it was getting harder to find happiness within myself.

I learned quickly that "sticks and stones will break your bones, but words will break your heart."

The bruises I had received could be easily hidden, but the damage he was doing to my heart was irreparable. I wanted so desperately to protect my precious sweet daughters! The more Jay yelled at them, the more I felt like a failure. I hoped that by redirecting his anger toward me, I would allow my daughters to find some happiness. So I started taking the blame for everything. I knew that I could take whatever Jay's punishments would be, but I couldn't bear to see my daughters pay the same price.

My days were filled with tears, and my nights were filled with the fear of having to do it all over again the next day.

It took only a few short months for me to realize that my life was doomed to be a struggle for survival and not a joy! I prayed each night that God would forgive me and give me the physical and emotional strength to survive one more day!

Chapter Five

One day Jay told me that if he had a child of his own he would be happier and would treat me and the girls better, so I wanted to become pregnant as soon as I could. I hoped that Jay would keep his word and we could all find some happiness in our home. When I found out that I was pregnant three months later Jay seemed really excited. He was sure that he was going to have the son he always wanted.

Again I went through this pregnancy alone. Jay was thrilled to be able to say he was going to have a son, even though we didn't know if it was a boy or girl, but he continued to be verbally cruel to me. He told me that I was getting even fatter and uglier as my child continued to grow inside me. It was only because I was the means by which he would receive his son that he found me tolerable.

I stayed inside the house every day and left only to get groceries, but even then it was only with Jay accompanying me. I had no friends and my world was only as large as my own yard. With no one around that really cared about me, I found it easy to not care about myself. I had quit wearing makeup because Jay wouldn't allow me to, and my red curly hair was pulled up into clips most of the time. I wore baggy sweatshirts and pants and tried my best to disappear into the background so that no one would see the pain I was going through.

Jay even accused me of going to too many doctor appointments even though I was only going once a month. He actually believed that the examinations were an excuse for me to spend time with another man. Despite the fact that he would wait outside the examining room he still wouldn't trust me.

One day when I was doing laundry I found what I believed to be a bag of pot in one of his drawers. I had never seen pot before, but I didn't know what else these leafy things could have been. I took it not knowing if I wanted to confront Jay with it or not, but just wanting him to know that I was aware of it. When Jay returned home and saw it missing he demanded to know where it was. I told him that I had thrown it away.

Jay became so angry that he tore the shirt right off of me and punched me in the face. I was still pregnant at this time. My face was swelling and my eye was turning black, but all he could think about was that I had stolen his pot.

This was the first time that I realized that when Jay became that angry his eyes turned from a hazel color to a bright green, almost fluorescent. It was very frightening!!

Needless to say I gave his pot back to him. I then grabbed my daughters and my car keys and ran for my car. We were able to get into the car and lock the doors before Jay caught up to us. Jay opened the hood of the car and ripped off the distributor cap so the car wouldn't start. This was before the days of cell phones, so I had no way of calling anyone for help.

I remember the look of hatred in his face as he screamed at me that he would kill me before he let me leave with his child, and I knew in my heart that he meant every word of his threat.

I sat in the car crying for what seemed like an eternity. I was so scared but I didn't know what to do. I knew that if I went back into the house the beating would continue, but I had nowhere else to go. So I gave Jay time to cool off and then sadly took my daughters back into the house.

This was the start of the "I'm so sorry game" that would be part of my life for years to come. Me being sorry for making him mad again, and him saying he was sorry for getting mad. He promised me that it would never happen again.

I knew that if I wanted to have any peace in my life I would have to try my best to forget what had happened and pretend that it never happened at all. But I knew after this incident that there was no hope of escape! I had seen the extent of Jay's determination to keep what he now had possession of, and I knew that he would never let me leave, not alive anyway.

Chapter Six

Because I was in labor with my daughters for only one hour, when I felt like I had started labor with this child the doctor admitted me into the hospital. It had been proven that the second child will often be delivered faster than the first.

I went into the hospital on the afternoon of July 20. By later that evening the labor pains had lessened, but the nurses told us that the doctor wouldn't be able to break my water until the next morning, and because I had already been admitted they couldn't let me leave the hospital. Although we had only been in the hospital for a few hours, Jay became very angry.

Jay's anger had become a daily routine that I had become accustomed to. I just knew that it would happen no matter what I did. He was angry at me this time for wasting his day off sitting in the hospital. He told me that he had better things to do than to waste time sitting there with me. He got up from his seat and yelled at me, "You can't even have a baby right!" He said that he was leaving and he would be back the next day. As he left the room he told me that I better not waste any more of his time and I better get it right next time.

Instead of lying in my bed dreaming of the beautiful child that was about to be born, I spent the night crying and feeling again…Worthless!

For the first time in years I truly prayed and asked God to change Jay. I told God that I knew I deserved everything I was going through, but I didn't want my sweet new child to have to live the same life my daughters were living. I prayed for forgiveness for all the terrible mistakes I had made and promised God that I would do everything in my power to make it right, if He would just give me a happy home to take my precious new child to.

I couldn't tell if God was listening; I just hoped with all my heart that it wasn't too late for me to find God's love again. I really needed Him to love me more than my earthly parents seemed to.

I desperately needed to believe that someone cared about me and wouldn't abandon me.

The next morning Jay returned just as the doctor was breaking my water, and forty-five minutes later my beautiful son Scott was born. He was born so quickly that the doctor hadn't even had time to return to the delivery room before he was born.

Scott weighed six pounds two ounces. He was a beautiful child, and I thanked my Father in Heaven for giving me a son. I'm not sure what Jay would have done if I had delivered a girl.

As Jay promised, our son became the light of his life. Jay was so proud to be the father of a son (as if creating a son made him more of a man.) However, now Libby, Rachell and myself were even more useless in Jay's eyes.

If Scott cried I was in trouble. And if he got sick I was really in for trouble, and even though the girls adored Scott, they were never allowed to hold him. It wasn't until Scott started crawling that Libby and Rachell were even allowed to play with him.

The girls and I loved Scott so much, and we were thrilled to have a reason for happiness in our home. Scott being all boy was into everything and climbing everything he could find. Libby, Rachell and I followed him around constantly to make sure that nothing happened to him. We didn't want to get in trouble if he got hurt.

Scott brought the girls and me great happiness, and we learned to have fun while Jay was gone. I remember watching the news one night where there was a story about a man that killed his wife and children and then took his own life. Jay turned to me and said, "If you ever leave me that is what I will do; I would kill all of you and then myself because I will never go to prison for someone as worthless as you!"

I truly believed he would do it! My fear of Jay consumed my every move. I could feel his eyes watching my everywhere I went. I felt like he was just waiting for me to mess up again so he could get angry.

During this time it seemed that every TV program was about women that were being mistreated by their boyfriends or husbands. The audience would always tell the women to just leave him. They had no idea that for me that was not a possibility. Just leaving would mean death for me and my children. I was willing to take the chance for myself, but I couldn't let him kill my children.

Because I couldn't "just leave" I felt even more guilty for the life we had to endure. With nothing changing I had to believe that God had turned his back on me for good. He must have decided that I wasn't worth the effort. Therefore I gave up on myself too.

I never had the strength to tell Jay "NO" to anything, so I found myself doing things that made me feel even more horrible about myself. And the guilt of those things were devastating to my soul.

Jay came to me one night and wanted me to smoke some pot with him. He tried to guilt me into it by saying that if I really loved him I would do it. I insisted that I would never do such a thing. If there was anything I could control in my life, this decision was the one that I would stand strong on.

The third time Jay tried to get me to join him, I was beaten for telling him no. After several more attempts on his part to get me to join him, and several more bruises, I finally gave in.

I can honestly say that I hated it! My head was spinning and I couldn't breathe. I had to run outside for air. Jay just laughed and enjoyed seeing me in a panic. Even worse, I hated myself for giving in and doing something that I never wanted to do.

This was just the start of allowing Jay to bully me into things that I didn't want to do. I could see that by giving in to him I started to hate myself even more. I didn't think I could hate myself anymore than I already did, and it continued to amaze me how far down my soul could really go.

Soon joining him for his pot sessions wasn't enough. He started to bring home pornographic movies which I was made to watch with him. They disgusted me and made me remember all the horrible things I had done in my past. I felt tortured by those memories, and again I thought that God was punishing me for the things I had done.

With hate for Jay and for myself, I gave in for the sake of not being hit. I learned to pretend that I was smoking the pot, and being part of his sexual fantasies was done with disgust and hatred on my part. I had learned that in order to survive I had to become oblivious to my feelings or they would consume me.

With each passing day I felt more degraded and disgusting. However, I wasn't strong enough to stop what had been started. I allowed these things to continue for the sake of keeping Jay happy in the hopes that he would not beat me anymore.

The worst part of all was that I was expected to tell him that I loved him each day; even though that was the farthest thing from the truth, I would do it.

It is amazing the things you will allow into your life when you feel "worthless"! When you believe that you are at the bottom, you don't feel like you can get any lower. Each horrible thing becomes another link in the chain that holds you down.

The daily struggle for survival continued for years. These years are more of a blur of emotions than real understanding. They were years of tears and pain that continued to wear my soul away to nothing.

On one occasion Jay became extremely angry because Rachell, who was only four, sucked her thumb while she was asleep. She didn't even know that she was doing it. Jay grabbed her from the bed and dragged her to the kitchen, where he pulled her hand and held it on the counter. He reached for a butcher's knife and screamed at her that he was going to cut off her thumb.

I frantically pulled at Rachell's tiny body trying to release her from his grip and screamed at Jay to stop. When I couldn't get him to let go of her hand I slapped him across the face. He let go of Rachell and with the look of a madman he turned to me and punched me in the stomach so hard that it caused me to fall to the ground and struggle for air. Jay then laughed and said, "That will teach you to ever touch me."

As much as I hated him at that moment I knew that I would never again have the nerve to stand up to him. And he knew that he had taught me not to interfere again.

This incident reminded me again that my life was not destined to have a "happily ever after" and that happiness would never again be a part of my life. I realized that my "ever after" was to be one filled with hopelessness and fear.

Chapter Seven

The year that Libby and Rachell began kindergarten was very exciting for me. I knew that they would get out of this house of fear, if only for a few hours each day. I wanted desperately for them to see that there were kind people in the world, and not everyone was unhappy all the time. I would put little notes into their lunch boxes saying "I love you! Have a great day!" I wanted them to know how special they were to me!

Jay had started finding ways to intimidate us daily. He never passed any of us without giving us a kick or shove to get out of his way. And he loved to tell us how stupid we were and the name calling became a daily routine.

One night Rachell and Scott were playing in Scott's room. When Scott started crying, Jay ran down the hall to see what was wrong. Rachell tried to tell Jay that Scott had swallowed a penny, but before she could finish telling him, Jay threw Rachell over the door gate and into a planter we had at the end of the hall.

I ran to sweep Rachell into my loving arms of protection, but was screamed at by Jay to leave her alone or I would be next. My fear of Jay was so strong that I couldn't even defy him for the sake of my own child.

I cried as much as Rachell did because I was the one that had allowed this "monster" to be in the same house as my precious children, and I felt completely helpless to change it. What kind of a worthless mother was I that I couldn't even keep my children safe in their own home? My desperate soul continued to cry out to God for vengeance. How could He allow these things to keep happening without stepping in to rescue us?

The next morning Rachell had a black eye. When she went to school her kindergarten teacher asked what had happened. She said simply, "My dad did it."

That afternoon the social workers were at our door. Jay told them that what had happened to Rachell had been an accident. Later in the conversation Jay admitted to them that he hit me occasionally but it was my own fault. I made him do it.

I knew that I was far from perfect, but I had never intentionally done anything to hurt anyone. And I certainly never tried to create a situation that would deserve being hit. Jay's comment cut into my heart. Did he really believe that everything was my fault?

By the end of our conversation with the social workers Jay promised them that the girls would be perfectly safe when they returned from school and there wouldn't be any more incidents. So they left without taking any further action. After they left, I of course paid the price for his embarrassment.

Jay knew that he needed to make sure that no one else was told of his behavior, so when Rachell got home he took her for a ride on his motorcycle and bought her some ice cream. Rachell told me later that night that Jay had told her, "Whatever happens in our home is nobody else's business."

We both knew exactly what Jay meant!

These sweet little girls were forced to learn how to hide their tragic lives from the world just as I did.

About six months later I was fixing dinner and I sent the kids to wash up, I could hear some commotion going on down the hall and went to see what was going on. I saw that Jay was kicking Libby but I didn't know why. I screamed at Jay, "Stop it! That is enough!" When I screamed at him he finally stopped and left the room.

After he left I held Libby and asked Rachell and Libby what had happened. Rachell told me that Libby was horsing around when she washed her hands and flipped some water at Scott. Scott started crying and Jay went to see what was going on. Scott told him that Libby had sprayed him with water and Jay flipped out grabbing Libby and throwing her across the room. He then started kicking her.

I told Libby how sorry I was for what had happened, then we all went to the dinner table and had to pretend like nothing had happened.

I was told by Rachell sometime later that she was very angry at me because she thought that my saying "that's enough" meant that I agreed with the punishment and only stopped Jay when I felt that Libby had enough.

It broke my heart to know that my daughter believed that I wanted these terrible things to happen to them. I didn't know how to tell them that I wasn't strong enough to take the chance that Jay would kill us all and run away with them.

Again I prayed for God to help my children understand that I truly did love them. I prayed that someday they would understand and forgive me!

The results of the abuse on Libby's and Rachell's lives are their stories to tell, if and when they are ready to tell them, but for me to watch it unfold was heartbreaking. The verbal and emotional abuse continued daily, and we all grew accustomed to it.

About this time I realized that I needed to go to work because the cost of everything in our lives was getting more expensive. With the girls in school and Scott in diapers we just weren't able to make it financially.

I wasn't sure how I was going to pull this off, I wasn't ever allowed to leave the house alone, but after several very heated arguments Jay agreed to let me get a job at the grocery store deli a few blocks away. I soon found out that he would sit outside and watch me through the front window to see who I was talking to and watch what I was doing. When I got home he would ask me who everyone was, and I was expected to remember every customer. If I smiled too much at anyone he wanted to know why.

I was the one responsible for paying the bills and making sure that the money wasn't wasted. I had to show Jay the receipts from everything I purchased. When the money was gone Jay would want to know where it had all gone. Even though he had seen every receipt, I was expected to remember every cent that I had used and was made accountable again to explain where it had gone. For me this was just another way for him to torture me. My brain couldn't keep up with everything it was expected to do.

My life was an emotional roller coaster, never knowing what was going to make Jay angry next. Sometimes it was just the fact that I was breathing. The one constant thing in my life was the knowledge that he would be angry every day. I had never in my life known anyone that got so much pleasure from causing others pain. I just couldn't comprehend it.

We decided to buy a mobile home and put our money to better use. We moved to a new city not far from where we were so that Jay was still close to his job. I started working at a small store that had large windows in the front by the check stands. Jay was working swing shifts at the wood-treating plant in town, and he was with the children while I was working early mornings.

Jay would sit in front of the store with Scott and watch me working. I always knew that he was there, so I was careful not to smile or talk to anyone. It made my job as a cashier very difficult.

I would go out to the car during my breaks and I was usually slapped for talking to some stranger that had been in the store. With a hand print on my face and tears ready to spill from my eyes at any moment, I had to return to work and try to make it through the rest of the day.

I knew something had to change! And I knew that I was the one that was going to have to make the change if it was to be done.

My mom and her third husband made plans to move to an apartment not far from where we were living. They would be working as apartment managers for their building. I was so excited to finally have someone close to me that I could talk to and share all my feelings with. However, when we did go to Mom's home, I could tell that Jay listened very close to everything I said. I was never allowed to be alone with Mom. Even when we went into the kitchen to fix dinner, Jay would turn down the sound on the TV so that he could hear what we were saying. Mom shared with Jay and myself the frustrations she was going through with her husband.

Mom's husband was being unkind to her and had started going into town to pick up prostitutes. Jay was always supportive of her, telling Mom that she should get out of the marriage. Yet I had to pretend that everything was just wonderful in our marriage.

I think that Mom was so involved with the troubles of her own life that she wasn't able to see the sadness in our lives.

About a year later Mom decided that she was ready to end her marriage. She came to stay with us while she looked for a new job and a place to live. I know that after being in our home for an extended amount of time she could see the troubles we were having. Mom tried the best she could to not cause waves. She would try to keep to herself while ignoring the anger she could feel in our home. I was, however, allowed to go to church with Mom and my children, and I felt peace while we were there, but I still didn't feel like I deserved to be there. I had made too many mistakes for God to ever forgive me. And the things I had allowed Jay to do to my children would forever be a reason for God to turn from me.

I can't blame Mom for not standing up for us and stopping Jay from being cruel to us. She was so much like me and she just didn't have the strength to confront Jay and take the chance of making him more angry. After spending several months with us Mom decided to go and visit my sisters for a while. She said that she felt like she was just creating more problems by being in our home.

I knew that Mom loved me, but still I felt like I wasn't special enough to fight for. I needed to make a change for all our lives, and I knew it had to be now.

I convinced myself that Libby and Rachell would be better off with their real father, Mitch. The girls were six at the time and though they didn't really know him as a father, I knew that they would be treated better by him than they were being treated here. I also knew that Scott would be alright with Jay. Scott was only three and I knew he would soon forget about me.

I wasn't really needed by anyone! I was powerless to protect the most important people in my life! And in my heart I felt that I was truly worthless and disgusting!

To describe how I felt at this time, I would have to say I felt hollow. I couldn't find happiness, and sadness was completely a part of my life. With no emotions of any kind I simply felt "hollow."

I didn't know how to feel happy or sad... I just needed to feel done!

I knew that if I woke up in the hospital someone would help me. And if I woke up in front of God, I prayed He would understand. God knew what I had been going through, and I just hoped that He would forgive me.

Even though I didn't feel worthy of God's love, I wanted to believe that He still cared.

Every night Jay would call the house at the same time on his lunch break. I was always expected to answer within two rings. After talking to him that night I tucked my precious Libby, Rachell and Scott into their beds and told them that I loved them so much! With tears in my eyes I told them that I was sorry I couldn't be a better mother to them.

With the sound of their sweet voices saying "I love you too, Mommy" still in my thoughts, I swallowed a handful of sleeping pills then lay down on the couch and waited to see what the outcome would be.

Chapter Eight

As I slowly regained consciousness I could smell the unmistakable smells of a hospital. I was extremely sleepy and could barely open my eyes. There was a nurse with me, and I could tell that there was a tube down my throat. The nurse asked me if I had all the bruises on my arms before the paramedics brought me in. I couldn't even think and didn't know what she was talking about. The last thing I remember before slipping back into a deep sleep is the nurse telling me that they almost lost me.

I woke up again to the sound of Jay's voice yelling at me because I had embarrassed him in front of the guys at work. Jay said that the only thing I had accomplished was embarrassing myself and him. He said that the amount pills I had taken wasn't enough to do anything other than make me sleep. His next comment was "You really can't do anything right, can you?"

For whatever reason, Jay had called home again later that night, and when I didn't answer the phone he left work and came home. Of course he just knew that he would come home and find me with another man, because in his mind that was the only reason why I wouldn't be answering his call. Instead he returned to find me lying on the floor.

I guess when the phone rang again I must have tried to get to it, but I don't remember. Jay told me that if anyone asked me what had happened, I was to tell them that I was just stressed out from work. He told me that if I said anything to embarrass him any further, I would be sorry when I got home.

When someone did come in to talk to me, Jay was standing right there next to the bed glaring at me. So of course I told them what I had been instructed to say. My heart fell when I realized that nothing was going to change. I never dared ask Jay how my body became so bruised. It didn't really matter anyway because he would have made up a story that made it my doing.

That was the moment that I realized I was truly all alone in this world. I knew I couldn't stop Jay from abusing me, but I was determined never to let him make me feel like I didn't want to live again.

I told the doctor that I would get counseling from the bishop at the church I was attending with Mom, so they let me leave the hospital. When I did set up a meeting with the bishop, Jay insisted on coming along. The conversation we had was between Jay and the bishop; I was never allowed to tell my side of the story. Jay told the bishop that I worried too much and let little things upset me, so I'd had sort of a nervous breakdown. The bishop didn't really know me because I had only been going to his church for a short time with Mom and I hadn't really talked to him before this time.

I wanted to be able to tell the bishop everything that our whole family was going through, but after the first meeting the topics of discussions turned to Jay's work and sporting events. I started to believe that maybe Jay was really capable of convincing the whole world that I was the one with all the problems. I just wanted one meeting with the bishop alone, but Jay was always with me.

I convinced the bishop that I would never try anything so

stupid again and ended the sessions. They weren't helping me to change the problems; if anything they were just giving Jay the opportunity to make himself look like an even greater guy.

Now Jay knew that no one at church would believe me, even if I were able to tell anyone the truth. So the abuse continued. I just had to learn to take it and not let it consume me anymore.

Mom called and asked me if I had taken the pills on purpose or if it had been by accident. I told her that it was done on purpose. She didn't know what to say except "I guess I should move out so I don't cause you any more trouble." What I wanted her to say was that she was going to take us away with her to somewhere safe, but Mom didn't have the strength to get us away from Jay's hold on us. It broke what was left of my heart when Mom left to live with Penny. I felt like I had been abandoned forever.

Days turned into years, and they were always the same. Threats and intimidation were to be expected in everything we did.

Several times after that event while having Jay's hands wrapped around my throat in rage I told him to just kill me. If he hated me so much, why not just get it over with. He never took it far enough to do any real damage, just enough to remind me that he was still in charge.

I continued to cover the bruises and prayed for the strength to survive. If Jay had wanted to kill me, I couldn't stop him, but I was determined to never let him bring me to the point of wanting to hurt myself ever again.

I had been raised going to church, and knew that was where I needed to be again. I felt a strong need to have God in my life again. I needed to know if God really did care about me. I was going to attend church every Sunday, no matter what it took. And I was going to make sure that my children were with me. I needed them to know that they really did have someone that loved them, and I prayed that God would let them feel his love!

It wasn't always easy. I had my dress torn from my body several times, but I went as often as Jay would allow me to. I accepted a position as a Sunday school teacher for the little children, and with the responsibility of needing to be there each week for my class, I knew we would have somewhere safe to go.

Occasionally Jay would go to church with us, but not because he wanted to be there. Instead it was to see who I was talking to and what I did while I was there. Jay was quick to remind me of all the horrible things I had done and that I was a hypocrite for going to church; it was his way of pulling me down and not allowing me to change. He still needed to feel in control.

I did feel like a hypocrite, but I was determined to change. I just knew that I could!

Jay never let me go anywhere alone; either one or all of my children were made to go with me, because of course, I couldn't be trusted. Even with them by my side, we were timed wherever we went. If it took us longer than Jay thought it should, we would be in trouble. We were in a world where we were walking on eggshells trying desperately not to break them.

Jay was in total control!! And we all knew it!

My personality had changed so much throughout those years. I didn't smile anymore, and I wasn't even ticklish anymore either. I wouldn't look people in the eye for fear that they would say something to me. If a stranger passed us on the street and said hello, Jay would demand to know who they were, and why they were talking to me? If I couldn't come up with an answer or told him that I didn't know them, Jay thought I was hiding something from him.

As my children grew older, I continued to attend church each Sunday with my children. I loved being with the little children in the Sunday school. They had so much love and tenderness that I craved in my dreary life. And with them I couldn't be accused by Jay of being with another man.

Another man was the farthest thing from my mind. I didn't even want the one I had. My life with men so far had not been worth the cost.

After teaching the children Bible stories for a few years I was given the opportunity to teach them music. I was able to find joy in the songs I would teach them each week. Even though I had always loved singing, I was never able to learn how to read music. I would draw picture posters of the words to the songs, and then I waited until I arrived at church to hear the melodies. I learned the songs for the first time along with the children.

Listening to their sweet voices would bring great joy to my soul. The Spirit of Christ was so strong in the room with us that my body would tingle. I was able to feel God's love returning inside me. The best part was that I could see that my children were feeling God's love for them and they were able to spend time with truly loving people at church.

As the years continued my children and I learned to have fun while Jay was at work. However, we could feel the atmosphere change in our home the minute he returned. I had always dreamed of a home where my children would all come running when Daddy came home, jumping into his arms and being met with love. The reality of our life, however, was that when Daddy came home everyone would run to their rooms to hide.

My precious children and I built what I call our "island of security." We were safe and relaxed with each other, and as the years passed we learned how to be supportive of each other. We played games and spent quality time together while we were alone. We were able to laugh and have a good time until Jay returned.

I tried to extend even more love to them in hopes of making up for the hard time they had to endure. I continued to pray that they could see my love for them despite the fact that I felt powerless to rescue them from our prison.

The bond we shared was one that could never be broken! We were the Four Musketeers…One for All, and All for One!!

Libby, Rachell and Scott were the love and joy of my life! And thankfully God had given them the wisdom to see for themselves who Jay was and to understand the hold he had on us all!

Chapter Nine

Jay grew up in a household totally different from mine. His father was a long-haul truck driver, and while his father was gone on the road for days his mother would always be accusing his dad of having affairs. Jay had an older brother and sister and one younger brother. The children were exposed to this world of distrust daily.

Jay's mother would abuse over-the-counter pain medications as well as prescription drugs, so she was unstable most of the time. In all the years I knew Jay's parents, I never heard them say one nice word to each other or about each other despite the fact that they remained married. That was what Jay learned about marriage, and he knew that love was a painful part of life. Accusations and mistrust were what he associated with a relationship.

I can't tell you much about Jay's childhood because he didn't share most of it with me. However, from the way Jay and his brothers behaved in their relationships I believed that they never felt loved in the proper healthy way that children should be loved.

His brothers treated their wives the same way that Jay treated me. So none of his family thought anything of the actions that Jay displayed while we were with them. Jay's sister Lynn left home at a very young age to escape from the anger of their home life. When she did visit, she didn't stay very long because her mother was always putting her down for something. Lynn's daughter Marie had been raised in Jay's parents' home, and Lynn would come to see her daughter more than anyone else. After Lynn had been insulted by her mother more than she could stand, she would just leave again.

Jay's father, James, would come to visit us about two times a year. He would stay for three to four weeks. The kids and I loved having him there. It became a reprieve for all of us. James needed to get away from the sorrows of his life, and we needed a buffer from the anger in ours.

I learned that James was a very kind, warm man. He had learned to not let all the bad things in his life get him down. He ignored all the negativity so that he could find peace in his life.

For years James had been working as a truck driver, but he was now part owner of the trucking company he had worked for earlier. I didn't know how he was able to do it, but he actually was able to be happy despite all the negativity he lived with.

Even though Jay was great about hiding all the abuse in our home from his family, I think that Jay's dad knew what was going on despite Jay's attempts to hide it. James and I would have long talks while Jay was gone to work. He shared with me the frustrations he had dealt with in his marriage, and the pressures he still faced. Even though he was able to share with me this very personal information, I still felt uncomfortable discussing our abusive lives with him. I still feared that Jay would find out that I had been talking about him and I would be in trouble. James never brought up the subject either, it felt like the "pink elephant" in the room. We both knew it was there, but we were unsure how to talk about it, so we never did.

I believe that James felt unable to change anything for us, but he learned to just be there with us. He came as a protector for me and my children, and there was peace in our home while he was there. We cherished the times we spent with him, and we were very sad when he left to return to his home.

Though I knew that James loved us, I also knew that Jay's mother would always take Jay's side no matter what Jay might do. On one occasion while Jay's parents were visiting us Jay became angry over something and started to yelling at me. When Jay left the room his mother, Rosa, came to me and said, "Honey, you need to try harder to get along."

I couldn't believe that she had said that to ME. After all I had been through, I couldn't even reply. I realized that Rosa believed Jay when he told them that all our problems were my fault. Her perfect son could do no wrong! Not in her eyes.

As the years of struggles continued, I would pray each day that God would change Jay. But nothing ever changed. One day in church, the speaker told us that if our prayers weren't being answered that maybe we were praying for the wrong thing. So I changed my prayers asking God to open Jay's eyes to see the way he was making us feel. I thought that if Jay truly understood the pain he was causing us, he would feel sorry and want to change.

However, after many years I realized that it wasn't going to happen. And if it had happened and Jay had been enlightened to how his actions were affecting us, he either didn't care or even possibly got great pleasure out of seeing his cruelty.

The years took their toll on my faith again and I started to doubt if God really cared or not. I was trying so hard to do all the things that God wanted me to do, and nothing was getting any better. I never doubted that God existed, I just didn't think He cared about me any more than my dad did.

I took a job working at a grocery store as head baker and part-time cake decorator. My work hours were from 4:00 a.m. until noon. In the deli connected to the bakery was a wonderful woman named Ann. She became the only friend I was able to have. Ann was the wife of one of Jay's coworkers. Ann and I became as close of friends as Jay would allow. The only reason Jay allowed me to be friends with Ann was because her husband Ken thought Jay was a wonderful man. We went over to their home a few time for barbecue dinners, and we put on the show of being a very happy family. We had all mastered this charade by this time. I wasn't able to share the details of our unhappy home with Ann because I knew anything I said would get back to Jay and he would take away the only friend I had.

To the outside world Jay looked like a very loving husband and father, but what was happening in the privacy of our home was a completely different story.

When Jay would sneak into the store to spy on me while I was working, Ann believed that he was coming in just to see me because he cared. She thought it was sweet that the loved me so much that he wanted to come and visit me at work. I didn't dare tell her that the only reason he was coming in was to find another reason to get mad at me. And he always found a reason. I wished every day that I would find the courage to tell Ann the truth. Every day got harder for me knowing that the world thought Jay was such a great guy. This only made the lie I was living even more painful.

Chapter Ten

Libby and Rachell were growing into beautiful young ladies. Libby had blonde hair and loving blue eyes. She had a great talent for art and loved to draw cartoons. Libby started making birthday and holiday cards for all of us. They were gorgeous! Even though Libby would put all her love into these cards, Jay couldn't find a way to encourage her efforts. He would find a way to turn them into something hurtful for Libby. Instead of telling her how lovely the drawings were, he would criticize her for misspelling words. Libby had the most heartwarming smile, but like me, Libby was very tenderhearted. Even though this was a wonderful quality, it also became a very cruel one.

Jay took advantage of the fact that he could easily make her cry. It seemed that Jay would focus on our strengths and turn them into weaknesses. It broke my heart to see him tear apart her feelings with his cruel words. The fact that Jay could get such a strong reaction from her made the two of us his prime targets most of the time. I tried my hardest to undo Jay's cruelty with my love for Libby.

Libby was becoming very withdrawn and tried to not be noticed for fear of bringing Jay's anger upon her again. I could see that the light she had in her soul was fading, and I wanted desperately to find a way to bring it back to her.

Her artistic talents continued to grow despite the negative words from Jay. I tried to encourage her and truly loved all the drawings she made. She had an incredible talent, and I wanted her to know that I could see it.

Rachell was a little stronger emotionally. She was able to stand up for herself a little better, but I could see that it was still painful for her when Jay would criticize her. She was able to hide her emotions better that Libby, and she didn't give Jay the reaction he was hoping for, so he didn't try as hard to tear her down

Rachell was also becoming a beautiful young lady, but very different from Libby. She had brown hair and sparkling brown eyes and stood about six inches shorter than Libby. You could tell that they were sisters, but you would never guess they were twins.

Rachell became very focused on her appearance. She would always be beautifully put together. Perfect makeup, great clothes and an attitude of pride in herself. That was the person that she showed the world, but I knew that in her heart she was still hurting from the unkind remarks Jay would throw at her.

Rachell learned to love music as much as I did. She had an incredible singing voice and would even sing solos at church from time to time. She would make me cry with pride when she sang; it reminded me of the years as a child when I loved singing and could do it with no fear.

Scott continued to be the joy of Jay's life. He really enjoyed riding and racing dirt bikes and was very good at it. I was nervous that he would get hurt, but he seemed to have a natural talent for riding and only fell a few times. He was involved in scouting and worked one summer as a camp counselor. Scott had a way of making everyone around him feel loved and accepted. However, as Scott became a young man Jay started being cruel to him also.

Scott would go out to help Jay with whatever he was working on and would soon come back into the house upset because his father would tell him that he was stupid and didn't know anything about what he was doing. Jay wouldn't even take the time to teach Scott; he would just send him away after insulting him.

By the time Scott was in the eighth grade he was taller than me. He had dark brown hair and loving brown eyes, and olive skin like his father. He was very handsome, and at close to six feet tall he was the tallest in the family.

Unlike his father, Scott was a very compassionate young man. He reached out to the people that were forgotten and left out by others. Scott wanted them to know they had a friend.

He also became very protective of Libby and Rachell. I know he wished that he could stop his father's cruelty to them, but he didn't know how. He tried to stand up on my behalf also, but would end up getting hurt for interfering.

I was working at the grocery store bakery and my hours at work were 4:00 a.m. till noon.

Jay worked 2:00 p.m. until midnight. I would come home from work and try to take a nap before the kids returned from school and then lie down on the couch for a few hours after they went to bed. I was expected, however, to get up and fix Jay something to eat as soon as he got home from work. I then was expected to stay up and watch TV with him until he was ready to go to bed. I was functioning on very little sleep.

Our house had a dishwasher, but we were never allowed to use it. Libby and Rachell were expected to wash the dishes by hand each night. It had now become a nightly routine for Jay to come home from work and inspect the dishes. If he found so much as a water spot on any of them he would throw them all back into the sink and drag whichever one of the girls had washed them out of bed and make them re-wash every one. After Jay finished screaming at them about cleaning the dishes he would start laughing as he watched them try to stay awake and re-wash the dishes until he decided they were done well enough for them to return to bed.

I tried whenever possible to wash them, but I was so tired myself that I couldn't help out very often. Again my heart would break as I watched Jay's cruelty. Jay also loved playing mind games with the children. If they were invited to a birthday party or school activity, he would tell them that they could go if they were good until the day of the party. They were always on their best behavior, but they would try extra hard not to make any mistakes so they would be able to attend these functions with their friends. Every time on the day of the party Jay would find something to get angry about and tell them that they couldn't go. Jay enjoyed setting them up for a fall. He did the same thing at Christmas time. We spent hours getting presents ready and setting up the Christmas tree only to have Christmas morning ruined by Jay screaming at us because we weren't opening the presents in the order he wanted us to or kicking us out of his way so that he could get to something. We could never get excited about any special event because we knew Jay would find a way to ruin it. Again I would question God as to why someone would get so much pleasure out of causing everyone else so much pain.

Each day continued to be a struggle to find happiness. The years seemed to go on forever. The year that Libby and Rachell turned thirteen, I was asked to be a Sunday school teacher for the young women. This would mean not only a class on Sunday, but also a mid-week activity. I knew that Jay would never allow me to do it because there would be other adults at the activities and some of them would be men. He believed that I couldn't be trusted around other men.

I had still been going to church each week and I felt safe with the little children. My faith was still very fragile and I didn't think I had the strength to take on this battle with Jay. I told them that I would pray about it and get back to them with my answer.

With fear in my heart, I did pray. The answer that came to my heart was that Jay would be mad no matter what I did, so I should accept the position. I called the young women's leader and told her that I would teach the classes. I didn't ask Jay for permission, I just told him that I was going to teach the class and then I waited for him to blow up. I knew I could take his punishment because I had so many times before.

As I started preparing the lessons and teaching these young women about how wonderful and special they were to God, I started to believe it myself. I started feeling God's love for me more deeply inside my heart. I soon realized that I was not there to save these girls, I was given this opportunity to save myself!

The more I told them about their self worth in God's sight, the stronger I became. It didn't take long for God's love to completely fill my soul. I felt for the first time in my life that I was someone truly "SPECIAL"! Someone loved more than I could ever know.

I was a daughter of my Father in Heaven and a precious child worth saving. I now knew that I was loved by my God and my Savior Jesus Christ!! I began listening to uplifting Christian music and could feel my strength grow as I drew closer to God. I understood how God could forgive me and still love me despite all the sins I had committed in the past. Having learned unconditional love for my children, I understood God's unconditional love for me.

I also knew that I needed these young women, especially Libby and Rachell, to really understand and know of God's love for them. I told them to never let anyone take the knowledge of God's love away from them. I warned them that there are many out there that will try and succeed if you allow them to. I needed them to know how important a good self-esteem is, and that it can be so fragile and easily broken. So protecting it is one of the most important things in your life. I wanted them to love themselves as much as God loves them.

I wanted them to understand that feeling good about yourself will help you through a lot of hard times. It will also help them make good decisions. More than anything they needed to truly understand that they are daughters of a God that loves them and knows how precious they are. And His love will always be with them, even if they make mistakes! I never shared with any of them the fearful life I was living. I couldn't tell them of my failures and mistakes. I just prayed that they could see in my heart that I knew from experience what losing your self-esteem could do to you.

I could feel God's strength and love with me each week as I spoke these words to the Young women. With passion in my heart, I kept telling them over and over how special they were, and I prayed that they would always remember what I was teaching them. I never wanted anyone else to have to live the way I was living.

In the fall before Libby and Rachell were going to graduate from high school I began to think that my life in Jay's prison would never end. I had survived Jay's torments for seventeen years, and even though my faith had grown enormously, I still felt like nothing at home was changing.

My daughters were looking forward to a future away from the world we lived in. Rachell had met a great young man and was planning on getting married shortly after graduation. I just prayed that she was truly in love with Artie, and not just looking for an escape from Jay.

I didn't get very many opportunities to get acquainted with Artie because Jay never allowed anyone to come into our home unless he invited them. And even then it was only until Jay decided that it was time for them to leave. I was only able to visit with Artie for very short amounts of time, but I knew his sisters from church and knew that they had come from a loving home.

I believed that they would be happy together and was extremely excited for Rachell.

Libby had made it clear that after graduation she wanted to move out also. She wanted to move into an apartment with her friends. She had no plans right away, but she knew that she had to escape from Jay's grips. I was so excited that my daughters would finally have a happy life, though I would miss them terribly.

It isn't necessary to dwell anymore on all the abuse that we endured for those seventeen years. It became a way of life that we grew accustomed to. In survival mode we didn't recognize it as abuse anyway; it just became a daily routine, and we had learned how to get through one day at a time.

Jay would never admit to having done anything wrong; after all, in his mind, every time he hit me or became angry it was my own fault. I made him do it. I always felt that things were going to change, I just never knew when or how. I did know that I needed to continue to survive until that day would come.

In October of 1996 Jay's sister Lynn came to visit us for a week. The kids and I were having a great time with her there. Lynn wanted to take us all to a movie, but Jay said that he didn't want to go. He tried to get me to stay home with him, but I told him that I wanted to see the movie and I was going even if he didn't. I knew when we left that Jay was already mad at me, but I went anyway.

After the movie we stopped to get some root beer and ice cream to make floats when we got home. Lynn decided to call her husband from the store pay phone before we returned to the house. Her conversation went on for quite some time, and the kids and I were getting very nervous because we knew that Jay was getting angrier with each passing minute. Lynn on the other hand had no idea that there was any problem so continued to take her time with the call.

As we turned onto the road leading to our house, Jay came driving toward us from the opposite direction. I stopped to tell him that we had gone to the store for root beer, but before I could finish what I was saying he started screaming at me wanting to know what had taken so long. As I parked the car in the driveway Jay came running up to me and grabbed the keys from my hand and hit me in the face with them.

Lynn yelled at him to stop hitting me, and Libby ran to him and for the first time in her life screamed at him, "If you ever touch her again… I'll kill you!"

Scott also yelled at his dad to stop and then ran off in tears. Rachell and I just stood there crying; we were shocked that he would do anything in front of his sister. He had always been very careful not to let his family see any of his abuse.

Later that night Libby told me that she thought she was going to die after yelling at Jay. She thought that he would come after her for standing up to him. What it did instead was stop him from hurting her anymore. Jay didn't know what to do when he couldn't intimidate her anymore.

Jay told his sister that he hadn't hit me. He said that I walked into his fist. I think Jay honestly thought that Lynn would believe his lie and take his side, but she had seen it for herself and decided to return home the next day because she didn't want to be around Jay anymore.

That night after Jay left for work I went to bed and started crying again. I was sure that there couldn't be any tears left inside me, but somehow they continued to flow.

I had cried enough tears in those seventeen years to fill an ocean!

With tears running down my face I looked up to Heaven and said, "God, I don't know what to do anymore. Please tell me what to do!"

It was almost instantly that I heard a voice in my head saying, "You've done all you can. It's time to get out."

I was so amazed! I had actually heard a voice that answered my prayer!

I didn't have any idea how I was going to get out, but if that was what God was telling me to do, then I knew he would give me a way to accomplish it. I was determined to do God's will!

I started looking for a means of escape. After thinking about it all night I decided that when Libby and Rachell graduated in the spring I would make my escape. I was going to find a train or plane and just disappear. That was the only way I could think of to get away. I knew that Jay would spend the rest of his life hunting me down. And if he did find me, he would kill me.

I knew that it would tear my heart out to leave Libby, Rachell and Scott behind not knowing if I would ever see them again, but I had to get out. And that was what I was going to do.

I trusted in God's words and prayed that He would find a way for me to be with my children again someday. I was willing to live in a cardboard box under a freeway, rather than stay in this house of fear any longer. I was almost forty and had lived almost half my life in Jay's horrible world. I wasn't going to waste any more of my life with him.

I told Libby and Rachell of my plans and Libby told me that she wanted to go with me. I was thrilled to have her by my side. I didn't tell Scott of my plans, not because I thought he would try to stop me, but because I couldn't take the chance that something would be said to Jay that would put an end to my escape. I knew that Scott wanted me to get away from his father. He had asked me several times why I let Jay treat me the way he did, but I couldn't tell Scott that I had allowed the abuse because Jay had promised to kill us all if I didn't.

Even though Scott thought I should get away, I knew that he would try to find a way to keep me there with him. And seeing my precious son in pain because of my leaving would have made me change my mind. I couldn't bear seeing the hurt that I would cause him. I prayed that Scott would forgive me in time and try to understand why I left him behind.

I tried to save any tiny bits of money I could for my escape, but Jay kept track of every penny that was spent. Hiding these small amounts was very difficult, but I managed to save about $100 in four months. Libby was also saving for our escape. I thought that by June I would be able to have around $200. I didn't know how far that would take me, but anywhere was better than here.

Before I could carry out my plan of escape God stepped in and changed my plans. He didn't want me running in fear for the rest of my life. He had a plan of escape for me that would free us from Jay's prison forever.

Chapter Eleven

In February of 1997, the year of Libby's and Rachell's graduation from high school, God set my future in motion. Jay's niece Marie and her family wanted to move to the state were we were living. She called Jay and asked him if we could come and help her move, and Jay told her that we would.

Marie had only seen the good side of Jay. She had been more of a little sister to Jay than a niece. The times she spent with our family growing up were ones in which Jay was on his best behavior. Jay would spoil her and treat her better than he treated his own children.

Marie was now a mother with a husband and son of her own and wanted to be closer to our family. Libby and Rachell were only four years younger than Marie, and they were as close as they could be for having lived 800 miles apart.

However, even Marie was never told of the fears we had in our home. She thought that we had a very happy family, and wanted to be near to us. The weekend we went to help Marie with her move Libby and Rachell had to work. They both had jobs and weren't able to get the time off to go with us. It was just Jay, Scott and myself that drove to help them.

Upon our return home we found out that Libby had invited some friends to the house. As I stated before, this was strictly forbidden! If anyone ever came to the house it was only with Jay's permission. This act of defiance on Libby's part was more than Jay could stand.

Jay hit the roof! He yelled at me that I was to call Libby at work and tell her to come home. I could see by the anger in his eyes that there would be real trouble if she did come home. I refused to call her and told him that it could wait until she was off work. I hoped that by the time she was finished working Jay would have cooled off.

That was not what he wanted to hear. Jay grabbed the phone and called her himself. He ordered her to come home and pack her bags because she was no longer welcome in his home.

I was surprised to see that Libby did come home as ordered. When she came into the house Jay started screaming at her and calling her every name in the book. He ordered her to get out of his house!

With God's strength flowing through my veins I looked Jay square in the eyes and said, "If she's going then I'm going too!"

He then yelled, "Go ahead and go!"

I grabbed Libby by the hand and said, "Come on, let's get out of here!"

Her reply was "But, Mom, I don't have any of my stuff." I told her that it didn't matter, we just had to get out of there now!

As we were running through the front yard toward the cars, Jay appeared on the front porch with his shotgun and the car keys. He threw the keys at me and hollered, "Take the car, you deserve it."

I looked at Libby and said, "Yes, I do deserve it." I ran for the keys not knowing if Jay would shoot me before I could pick them up.

I could see the fear in Libby's eyes when she saw the gun. I told her that I was either going to die or get out of this place forever. Either way we were going!

Rachell had gone out for the night with Artie, and Scott was at Marie's house visiting with her family so neither one of them had to see the danger we were encountering that night.

As we drove down the road Libby pulled her car off to the side of the road and ran back to my car. She told me that she didn't have any gas in her car and that she would need to stop at the next gas station. Even though I feared that Jay was close behind us, I told her to stop at the next station in town.

I guess the gas station attendant must have sensed that something was wrong because he came out to our cars and asked if everything was alright. I told him that I had just left my husband and that he had a gun. I was afraid that he was following close behind us. The man stood there with us phone in hand ready to call the police if Jay did catch us. When we were finished he wished us luck and we left the station.

I didn't know where to go or what to do. I had no friends, and the money I had been saving was still at the house. It happened to be a Sunday so I drove to one of our church buildings with Libby close behind me.

I wasn't sure what I would do when I got there, I just felt drawn to the church building. It just so happened that my future son-in-law's parents were walking out of the building as we pulled in. It was about 9:30 at night, but there was a late meeting that Artie's parents had attended.

I barely knew them, but I told them what had happened. They didn't know about our home life either. They had never been to our home but could see the fear in our faces and wanted to help. They told us to come over to their home and they would make sure that nothing happened to us. I told them that Jay would be looking for us, and anyone that would be helping us would be in as much trouble as we were.

They assured me that everything would be alright and made arrangements to hide our cars before we went to their house. I didn't sleep at all that night for fear that Jay would find us. After all, he had made me believe that if I left he would kill me, and I never doubted that he would follow through with his threat.

I was even more afraid that when Jay did find us he would kill everyone in the house just for helping me.

Jay knew that I had work the next morning, and I was sure that if he didn't find me that night, he would be at my work the next day. I was terrified to go to work, but with no money to my name and nowhere to live, I had to go.

None of my coworkers knew what I had been living with at home. I had become a professional at hiding it. I learned how to smile each day and pretend that my life was happy. There wasn't anything that could be done to change it, so I wanted to avoid the shame of letting others know that these things were happening.

I learned to keep my life a secret! After seventeen and a half years I was good at it!

The hard part now was that I would have to admit my weaknesses and failures to my coworkers. I was working at a daycare at the time and I went in early to tell my boss what had happened. I told her that I knew Jay would be coming in sometime during the day. I also assured her that I wouldn't let him do anything in front of the children.

When Jay arrived as I knew he would, I told him that we needed to go outside. The other teachers all watched out the front window, ready to call the police if anything happened.

When I got outside Jay handed me a bouquet of flowers and started once again the "I'm so sorry" game that he had mastered so well. I listened to Jay as he told me how sorry he was and promised (as always) that it would never happen again! He assured me that he would really change this time and he would be a better person.

I could feel the strength of God's power flowing through me as I stood face to face with Jay and without the slightest fear told him that I was glad he was sorry, and glad that he was going to change, but I was not coming back! At that moment I knew that Woman number three had broken free of her chains and would never be in prison again!

I know that Jay could see in my eyes that I had changed and I would never again be under his control.

Jay left angrier than before and sped down the street as he left. Libby, Rachell and I were able to stay with Marie while I tried to find a place for us to live. It seemed that all the apartments in town were renting faster than I could find them. I didn't want to move very far from town because the girls were still finishing school and Scott had decided to stay with his dad.

Scott told me that his dad needed him; I had the girls with me and Jay didn't have anyone. I knew that Scott would be safe with his dad, but I also knew that Jay would take this opportunity to try to turn Scott against me. I knew the relationship I had with Scott was one built on love and respect, but I feared that Jay's poison might get through to Scott's fragile soul and make him angry at me for hurting his father.

I soon learned that Scott had chosen to stay with his father because he wanted to protect me. He knew that if he came with me Jay would be there causing trouble for me all the time, and Scott didn't want to bring any more trouble into my life.

I once again had proof that God had given me a "miracle" in my son. Scott was a young man that loved me enough to endure living in a bad situation for the sake of my protection.

Chapter Twelve

After staying in Marie's home for about a week I found a newspaper ad for a townhouse right across the street from the daycare I was working in. Even though the ad was a week old I called about it anyway. To my amazement it was still available.

I could see again God's hand in preparing my way! With Libby's help we were able to pay the down payment and rent the townhouse. The first person I called was my mom. I told her how much I had missed her and missed being part of our family. We spent several hours talking, and I shared with her everything that had happened. I promised her that I would never leave the family again. She told me how proud she was of me and apologized for not being able to help me out of my situation. I assured her that she had nothing to be sorry for. None of us knew how to fix the problems I had. I just had to wait until God prepared me and led me down his path.

As the days went by I heard about the threats Jay had been making about taking his own life. He told Scott that if he ended up dead it would be my fault. I approached Scott and told him that if it did happen I would be sad, but it would not be my fault. It would be a choice that Jay made himself.

Libby also told me that Jay was making her believe that my leaving was her doing. I tried to make her understand that her actions that week and Jay's reaction to them were part of God's plan for giving me a way out of my prison.

I told her that God didn't want us running in fear for the rest of our lives. He wanted us to be able to live anywhere we chose and not be afraid of Jay any longer.

Libby asked me if I was afraid that Jay would come back and hurt us, and I told her that if he had intentions to do that, there was nothing I could do to stop him, but if I continued to worry about it then Jay was still controlling me. And I wouldn't let him control me anymore.

It was February when I left Jay and his hold over me, and the stores had all their Easter decorations on display. I was in the store looking at the decorations when a rush of fear came over me. My thought was that I had been gone too long and I needed to hurry and leave. That was the first real moment that I realized the changes in my life. I giggled to myself and thought, "I can stand here all day if I want to!" And I continued to browse, something I hadn't done in years.

I started telling my story to a few people at church. I had to admit to them all the horrible things we had been living with for so many years. I also told them about how God had emotionally and spiritually prepared me and then put into place the events that had led to my escape.

The next thing I knew some of the church members were bringing furniture to my apartment. They had rallied together to collect items no longer being used by them and brought them to my new home. They even gave me a washer and dryer, a TV and a microwave. None of the furniture in my home matched, but it was the most beautiful furniture in the world because it was given to me out of love. The best thing of all was that now my home was a place of peace and love. We had true joy for the first time!

God showed me once again how his hands were reaching out to me for my every need.

A short time later I was told at the daycare that we had a mandatory meeting after work; we were all expected to be there. To my great surprise they had planned a housewarming party for me and they gave me everything that I would need for my kitchen, even a table and chairs. The tears I was crying now were the greatest tears of joy! The outpouring of love I received was incredible!

I could see within myself that I had indeed become a new woman! I knew that with God by my side I could do anything!

After telling my story to one of the leaders from my church he looked at me with a tear in his eye and said, "What a leap of faith!" I had never before seen it that way, but I realized that he was correct. God told me to leave, and with no questions asked, I threw myself into his arms trusting that he would hold and protect me no matter what I may need.

I was so grateful to know that my Father in Heaven was carrying me, and I knew that He would never let me fall!

I had within me now a new strength and confidence that I had never felt before. My faith in God and my strength in myself grew as time went on.

I can't say that everything was easy after that point. I worked two jobs and still needed Libby's help to pay the bills, but we were happy. And I never worried about how to take care of things because I knew that the Lord was watching over us! Everything I needed seemed to find its way to me.

I hadn't realized how much of me was gone until I got it back. I could smile again. I could laugh with all my heart. And I was free to go anywhere I wanted, whenever I wanted to. God had freed me from my prison!!

Rachell was preparing for her wedding, which was planned for the week after graduation. Because I was unable to financially help her with the arrangements Artie's parents jumped in to help. I was so excited to be with her while she picked out her wedding dress and chose the bridesmaids' dresses.

Rachell invited all of Jay's family to the wedding and graduation because they were really the only family she had known while growing up. She also invited my mom and my sister Penny and her family. Penny's family came for the wedding along with Mom. Penny even made the wedding cake, and Mom made the bouquets and flower arrangements. It was wonderful being part of my own family again!

On the day before graduation Jay came to my apartment and tried to force his way in. I used both hands to push him by the chest out of my doorway and ran to the kitchen to call the police.

Jay left, and when he returned home he told his parents that he wasn't going to the wedding or graduation because I had physically abused him and I would make a scene if he attended.

Jay's parents had driven 800 miles to attend these two events with my daughters, but Jay made them feel so sorry for him that they refused to come. Jay's parents were the only grandparents my children had really known while they were growing up, so Libby and Rachell were devastated when they learned that their grandparents wouldn't be there for their graduation or wedding.

Again through the mind game that Jay played so well his family believed that everything was my fault.

Although I was hurting for my daughters I had a wonderful time at the graduation. It was the first time that I didn't need to worry about running into Jay. I found that I could laugh and have fun in public for the first time in years.

My first husband, Mitch, Libby and Rachell's father, had come for the graduation and wedding also. This was the first time I had really spent any time with him since our divorce. Libby and

Rachell would go to visit him during the summer, but they flew back and forth most of the time. They told me that while they were visiting their father they were mostly used as babysitters for his other children. Mitch would use this time to go on vacations with his wife, so they barely knew him as a father. Still they were happy to have him with them for these events.

Mitch and I were seated together for the graduation ceremony. I felt very uncomfortable, and I'm sure that he did also. I didn't want this uncomfortable feeling to continue, so I asked the girls for Mitch's hotel information and told them that I would like to talk to him if he would let me.

The next day I called Mitch and asked him if I could talk to him before the wedding. I could tell by his voice that he was completely caught off guard by my request. We agreed to meet at his hotel that afternoon, and Libby and Rachell came along prepared to swim in the hotel pool while Mitch and I talked. They were concerned about how the conversation would go.

I wasn't sure exactly what I was going to say, but I needed him to understand how sorry I was for all the pain our daughters had lived with. I told him that I was sorry for all the hurt I had caused him in the past and asked for his forgiveness.

Mitch told me that during their childhood he had thought of taking the girls away from me, but he knew that they were my life and I needed them with me. I thanked him and told him that I would have never made it if it weren't for my children. I told Mitch that I couldn't change the past, but I wanted to change the future for the girls. I wanted for us both to be able to get along for their sake. I told him that there would now be family events when we would both be together, and I never wanted Rachell or Libby to feel like they couldn't invite either one of us because the other would be there.

Mitch agreed, and the tension we had been feeling simply went away. We had a very nice time catching up on events of his family. It was great to know that we had both grown past the point of blame and hurt and could be comfortable with each other.

As I was leaving with the girls we had a great discussion about the future, and we were all happy to know that our family functions would be fun for everyone.

Rachell's wedding was beautiful! I felt wonderful being the mother of the bride. Rachell was so beautiful, and Artie glowed with love when he looked at her. A few days later I received a call from Marie and she told me that even though I would always be her aunt and she would always love me, it was too hard for her to spend time with me because Jay would get angry at her if she had contact with me. I told her that I completely understood and that Jay was her family and she needed to do whatever it took to keep peace in her home. I told her that I would always love her and if she ever needed anything she was welcome to come to me.

The time I was able to spend with my children was precious to me. We all had been able to put our past behind us and have fun in the present. After a few months Jay could see that his threats no longer had any effect on me, and he moved on to another victim. I felt sorry for this new woman; I feared that the treatment we had experienced would now be inflicted upon her. I could only hope that she was stronger than I had been and better able to protect herself.

A few months later Rachell was pregnant with my first grandson! What a precious gift of new life this was for us! Being able to go through the joys of Rachell's pregnancy made up for what I didn't have with mine. I was with her when she was shopping for the baby clothes and furniture and got to watch her tummy grow and wiggle with the new life inside her.

We had so much fun preparing for the birth of this precious child. We all felt like our future had great things in store for us.

As we were speeding to the hospital on the day Rachell went into labor, I was pulled over by a police officer for following too close to the car in front of me. I was the last car behind Scott, who was following Libby, Rachell and Artie in Artie's car. I explained to the officer that we were on the way to the hospital for the birth of my first grandchild. He chuckled and said, "Well, if you're going to rear-end anyone, at least it will be family."

He asked me to be careful and let me leave with a warning. It was great fun being part of the whole situation and it gave me a wonderful story to share with my grandson. At the hospital I reassured Rachell that because my labors had been so easy, she would also have an easy labor. After all, that was what I had heard. I was wrong! After being in labor for ten hours Rachell had to be taken into surgery for a c-section.

I found out that I was not the person to be trusted with the video camera. I was allowed to go into the delivery room with Rachell and Artie. After Artie instructed me to hold down the button on the camera we went into the room. I faithfully pushed the button while the doctor did the surgery. I filmed them taking my precious grandson to the warming table where Artie cut the cord. My finger was getting a cramp in it, but I wasn't going to let go of the button.

What a beautiful miracle Hayden was! He was a big baby, weighing eight pounds ten ounces. He had the most beautiful blue eyes and a darling button nose.

I was so excited! When we returned to Rachel's room for the rest of the family to see the birth I found out that I needed to release the button I was faithfully holding in order for the video camera to record. Needless to say, none of it was recorded.

It became a running joke that I was not to get anywhere near any video cameras.

Hayden's birth was such a great beginning for our new lives!

Chapter Thirteen

I had always dreamed of being a flight attendant even though I had only ever been on one airplane while growing up. I think all the years of moving during my childhood instilled in me a need to be on the go. The idea of exploring the world was fascinating to me. I decided that with my newfound strength and determination I was going to try now to live this dream.

I interviewed with a few airlines but wasn't hired at that time. However, I felt good about my efforts and knew that it was only a matter of time, and as I now knew, it was God's time and not mine. I knew that I would try again when I felt ready.

I used this time to reconnect with my family. My sister Penny invited me to go to Hawaii with her family and our mom. Mom had just gone through another divorce. We both saved everything we could so that we would be able to go.

My trip to Hawaii was wonderful!! Mom and I hunted for seashells and spent a lot of time sharing all the hurts we had gone through. I found out that in those years that I was lost to them that Mom had been going through some of the same things in her life. She felt bad about not being able to help me through my years of despair.

She loved to hear me tell her of how God had prepared me and then led me down the path to my freedom.

Mom and I built a great relationship through our faith! We explored and laughed and had the most wonderful time we had ever had together. I was not able to tell Mom how I had felt as a child. I was just grateful to be "special" to her now. No good would have come from making her feel guilty for things I felt as a child. There was no way to change it, so it was better left in the past.

She told me that my strength had given her the courage to make changes in her life. She told me for the first time that she was proud of me!

After returning from Hawaii I spent time getting to know who I was again. Libby and I lived together for two years, and we spent this time healing the hurts that we had been holding onto. I realized that she never blamed me for the things that were happening in our home. She knew that I was just as trapped as they were. This lifted a heavy burden from my soul; I was grateful to know that my children still loved me in spite of my weaknesses.

I was surprised one day when I answered a knock at my door and found Marie standing on my porch. She gave me a huge hug and said that she had missed me. She then asked me if I had a restraining order against Jay because she had gone to file one and was told that she could be included on mine if I had one. I asked her if everything was alright and she told me that Jay had become very possessive of her and was trying to control her life. She said that he tried to hit her three times.

I could see the pain in her eyes after learning what a monster her uncle was. She had loved and respected him so much and was devastated to find out his true nature. She asked me why I had never told her about all the horrible things he had done. I told her that she wouldn't have believed me any more than the rest of her family did. She had to see it for herself in order to really understand. A few short weeks later Marie and her family moved to another state to get away from Jay.

Two years after leaving Jay my children started living their own lives as all children do, leaving me with more time to myself. I decided that I would like to have a friend to go to movies with or out to dinner. I was working graveyard shifts 6 p.m. to 6 a.m. at a silicon wafer treating plant and didn't have much time to socialize. One of the radio stations in our area started a dateline and I thought I would try it out. I met several really nice guys, but I let them know that I was just looking for friendship. I had no intentions of getting into another relationship. I was honest and told them up front that if they expected sex after the date, they could look elsewhere because I wasn't part of that dating scene. When I first spoke to Ben on the phone he knew my intentions were only to be friends. He was fine with the idea and we decided to meet for coffee.

Ben was six feet three inches tall and was built like a mountain man. Even though he looked intimidating you could see kindness in his blue eyes. Ben and I started spending time together on my days off, and I thought we would continue to be good friends. Ben even suggested that we take turns paying for the dinners and movies so that it would be fair to both of us. I agreed and paid every other time for whatever we were doing.

I decided at this time that I really did want to work for the airlines, so I interviewed and was accepted for a position as a ticket agent at the airport. I knew that God would let me know when I should try for flight attendant again. I loved my job at the airport and the people I was working with. I was in a new and exciting world, and I loved each day that the Lord was giving me!

My mom came to visit us in October of 1999, and she was able to spend some time getting to know Hayden. He was her first great-grandchild. As we all did, Mom fell instantly in love with our precious Hayden. We all decided to go to the state fair, and I invited Ben to come along. Mom thought that Ben was a very kind man and was happy that I was out having fun again.

While we were at the fair Mom bought two large blue marbles. Mom gave one of the marbles to Rachell and told her that they were special because they would both have one. They could think of each other whenever they looked at the marbles. I remember Rachell telling me that she thought it was silly that Mom had paid $1.00 for each of these marbles, but Grandma loved the way the light shined through them.

I was so grateful for this opportunity to spend time with Mom again. Whenever we were together we had so much fun and spent most of our time laughing and just enjoying each other's company.

The very next month on November 12 Penny called me late at night to tell me that Mom had passed away. I was so shocked! I couldn't believe that Mom was gone. I had just gotten her back in my life, and I only had two short years to reconnect with her. She died very unexpectedly and way too soon. She left us when she was only sixty-three.

We didn't really know the reason for her death, but the coroner said that it was a severe asthma attack. Mom had never had asthma before, and I couldn't understand how it could just take over her life in a matter of weeks. I knew that if my memories of Mom were only those of how she died it would be a great dishonor to the incredible life that she lived. I knew that knowing what took her away from us would not bring her back, so I had to focus on all the wonderful memories I had of her while she was in my life.

My mom was not her death... She was her life! In the sixty-three years that my mother was on this Earth she touched a great number of lives. She brought joy to everyone around her and taught me that there is beauty in everything. Sometimes you have to really look hard, but you can find it if you truly want to. Mom radiated love and beauty! She definitely made this world a better place for her being in it!

After Mom's death I remembered her telling me that she felt her brother Wayne in the car with her a few weeks earlier. Wayne had passed away six months before this incident, but she said that she could feel him in the seat next to her and she reached over and touched the seat telling Wayne that she loved him.

She said that she knew she could tell me because I was the only person that wouldn't tell her she was crazy. I believed her story at the time she told me, but I was even more certain that it was true after she passed away. I believe that Uncle Wayne had come to take Mom home with him. Mom had told me on several occasions that if anything ever happened to her, she wanted me to sing at her funeral. Of course as her daughter I was sure that I would never need to because she was always going to be with me. When the time came to fulfill my promise to Mom I wasn't sure that I would be able to do it without falling apart. I did, however, agree to conduct the music during the funeral and sang as best I could for Mom. I know that she heard me, and I felt very proud to be able to share my songs with her one more time.

After Mom's funeral Rachell reminded me of the blue marbles and asked me if I would get the matching one for her. Even though at the time Grandma had given it to her it was just a marble, she now said it was the most precious gift she had ever received. I was able to get the marble for her, and they have become a wonderful reminder of Mom's love of nature.

In the last years that Mom and I had together, Mom would end every conversation with me by telling me how much she loved me and how proud she was of me! I knew that I had become someone "special" to her.

I never got angry at God for taking Mom away from me so soon after we finally found each other again. Instead I thanked Him for the time He allowed me to spend with her. Had I not been directed away from the cruel world I was in, I would never have had those last two years with my mother.

I knew that God had a plan, and His plan was to give me some precious memories of Mom to carry with me through the rest of my life.

I did wonder, however, if I really was as strong as God thought I was.

Chapter Fourteen

In April of 2000 my dad called to say that he and his wife wanted to come and visit me and my children. The thought of getting to visit with him after so many years was wonderful! Dad was married to his third wife, but she wasn't very kind to Dad. She only wanted what she could get financially from him. I met her for the first time at Mom's funeral. She pretended to be nice to my sisters and myself, but none of us really liked her. I was pleased to find out that Dad still cared enough about Mom to attend her funeral.

I was thrilled at the thought of Dad coming to spend time with me, but I soon found out that his wife just needed to use my flight benefits to get closer to her grandson that was living just two hours from where I was.

After spending one day with us they drove to see her grandson for the rest of the week. I saw them again briefly before they flew back home. I really needed to know if Dad wanted to be a part of my life again. I hoped that he did. The short amount of time we had for any real discussion never gave me a chance to find out what I really wanted to know.

The next month in May I got a call at work telling me that Dad had a stroke. Penny, Peggy, Sheri and myself flew in to see him in the hospital. Even though he was hooked up to a breathing machine and not conscious at the time, I'm sure that Dad knew we were there

The next morning he was awake and he responded to our questions and did his best to communicate with us that he was glad to see us there with him. The doctors told us that Dad would be paralyzed on one side but with rehab he could get a little better. My sisters and I decided that we would go ahead and return to our homes until Dad was ready to be transferred to a rehab facility.

We decided that we would each take turns coming to help Dad with his recovery. We all knew that his wife wouldn't do anything for him, she was too selfish. The night before we were to return home I asked my sisters to pray with me, and I asked God to give us all the strength to accept His will for Dad, whatever it might be. I knew it wouldn't be easy for any of us. We left on Saturday night with a plan for the next few months of care for Dad.

The next morning Rachell called and asked me to come over to her house. Penny had called Rachell instead of me because she knew she would fall apart if she talked to me. When I arrived Rachell told me that Dad had died that morning. She said that Dad had waited for us all to leave before he passed on.

I called my aunt Anita, Dad's sister, and found out that after we left Dad slipped into a coma. His wife then decided to pull the plug on the respirator and let him go. Dad's wife never called anyone in the family to tell us what had happened. Not even Aunt Anita, who had been there every day visiting Dad.

Aunt Anita had just happened to walk into the room as Dad passed away. She had no idea what she was walking into. I wouldn't have stopped his wife from letting Dad go, but I would have liked to have the opportunity to be with him when he died.

Because Dad died the weekend of Memorial Day most of his

close friends were out of town. His wife was extremely angry that there weren't more people at his memorial service. The fact that they weren't there for Dad wasn't what upset her; she was angry that they weren't there to take care of her.

After Dad was buried his wife wouldn't even pay for a marker to be placed on his grave. Aunt Anita tried for a year to get his wife to purchase a plaque but finally got frustrated and ordered it herself.

In all of my memories I can't remember my dad saying to me the words "I love you." His response to me when I told him that I loved him was "Thanks, I appreciate that."

I knew that he loved me the best way he knew how, but I wanted to hear him say it. I have never asked my sisters if they got the same response as I did. I guess I never really wanted to know just in case I was the only one he couldn't say it to.

Though my parents were divorced years earlier, they never were able to find true happiness again in the other relationships they had.

I believe that they needed to be together again. And now they are! And I know I will be with them both again someday!

Chapter Fifteen

Ben started trying to get me to change my mind about dating him; he wanted our relationship to become more than friends. I was still shying away from relationships even though I knew that God had changed me. I wanted to be careful not to lose myself again. There were several issues I was being very cautious about.

I told Ben that if he ever made me choose between him and my children that he would lose. And that I would never allow anyone to take "me" away from me again. Even though Ben assured me that those things would never happen after a short amount of time I started to see signs that made me uncomfortable. I truly believed that I was strong enough to not be taken in by another person's insecurities, but I soon found myself changing to try to please Ben.

Ben wanted me to commit to dating him exclusively even though I wasn't seeing anyone else. It was important to him that I say it. I would ride around with Ben in the dump truck that he owned and used for his job, and we would talk for hours as he worked, getting to know each other better. Ben continued to be very kind and co-signed for me to buy a car and a mobile home. He never actually put any money into them because I faithfully made every payment on time. However, Ben made it a point to tell everyone about his generosity. He wanted everyone to think that he had gone to great lengths on my behalf.

Because I had been told so many times during my marriage to Jay that my smile was horrible, I decided to get braces to straighten out my teeth. My insurance with the airlines would pay for all but $200, so I decided to go ahead and have them put on.

The orthodontist would accept payments until the balance was paid off, but Ben insisted on lending me the full amount up front, saying that I could pay him back when I got the checks from the insurance company. It sounded like a very generous offer until Ben started hounding me for the payments. If the insurance company didn't pay on the day Ben thought it should, he had me call to find out where the payment was.

I very quickly regretted letting him pay for it in advance. This was when I found out that Ben was the kind of man that would do anything for you, but then you owe him. And if you aren't grateful enough or don't recognize his generosity as often as he thinks you should, he would remind you that you were in his debt.

I felt like I wanted to put a stop to our relationship, but Ben made me feel like I was too indebted to him to walk away. I tried to distance myself from him by spending my days off at home instead of with him. Ben would make me feel guilty, wanting to know why I didn't want to be with him. I told him that I just needed time to myself, but he would sulk and tell me that I didn't appreciate everything he had done for me. He asked me to move in with him, but I told him that I wasn't going to "play house" with him.

Scott was now living with his girlfriend Dana. They came over to visit me and told me that Dana was pregnant. Scott told me that he had been afraid to tell me because he thought I would be angry. However, I told him that I was thrilled! I couldn't wait to have another precious grandchild in the family.

At this time I decided to try again to become a flight attendant with the airline I was working for. I worked sixteen hours a day saving the money I would need to get through the five weeks of unpaid training.

This also gave me an excuse to spend more time away from Ben. After four months of long hours I had saved enough to get me through the training. With three of my coworkers I went to the interview, where we were all hired, and we all prepared to go to the training together. I was so excited! I was finally going to live me dreams!

MaryAnn, Joann and Verna became my dear friends during training. We had so much fun together studying and drilling each other on questions to make sure that everyone would make it through the intense process.

Ben came for my graduation from flight school, where he told me of his concerns that I would not be able to spend as much time with him if I had to fly around for my job, but he assured me that he would support me because he knew it was what I wanted.

The day before I was to fly my very first official flight Scott called me to say that Dana had gone into labor. The baby wasn't due for another six weeks so I was out of town and not able to be there for his birth. I could hardly wait to get home to see him.

Rylan was born on November 29, and he was a beautiful baby! He looked just like Scott, with big black eyes and olive skin weighing six pounds two ounces. I could see the joy in Scott's eyes; he was so excited to be a father. I knew that Scott would treat this child with love and respect and never become the monster that his father was.

My life was so blessed that I could hardly contain my excitement. Not only was I living my dream I also had two wonderful grandsons to share my dreams with!

After I started flying I began to see changes in Ben. He started trying to get me to spend more time with him. He wanted me to be with him whenever I wasn't working, but it was always my responsibility to go to him.

I felt like Ben thought his time was more valuable than mine. In his mind if I loved him I should want to go out of my way to be with him. I wanted to spend more time with my grandchildren, but Ben made me feel guilty if I didn't choose to be with him. I had to drive forty-five miles one way to be with Ben, and I realized that I was giving in to him just to make him happy. However, I was making myself unhappy.

While I was with him we were either driving around in his dump truck while he worked or I was sitting in his shop while he worked on the truck. There were very few times that he actually stopped working to just be with me. He could always find things that needed to be done. He never had time to travel with me or to drive to my house to spend time with my family. I was expected to go to him.

We invited him to several family events but he was always too busy to attend. I learned that I couldn't worry about him feeling left out because he was choosing to exclude himself from these events.

My job required me to be on call, and I had to be ready to report at the airport within two hours of being called out. On the days that I was on duty I had to stay close to home so that I would be ready if they did call me. This made it harder for me to spend the time with Ben that he wanted me to.

I learned that each day I was at work God would give me opportunities to reach out to others and bring happiness into their lives, even if it was for only a few hours. I started looking forward to those moments when God would show me that I had touched a life in a special way. I didn't question where He would send me because I knew that there would be a reason for my being there.

One trip was supposed to take me to Chicago, but after misconnecting in Seattle I was sent to Long Beach, California. I told the other crew members that I believed there was a reason for being re-routed, I just didn't know what the reason was yet.

The next day after walking around for a few hours I headed back for the hotel. I had a feeling that I should turn down a side street I had been on only a few minutes earlier. A short distance down the road I saw two young boys standing on the corner looking back towards the building.

These boys were very nicely dressed and looked distressed. As I approached them I looked to see what they were looking at. I noticed a young lady lying over the top of a garbage can. I asked the boys if they knew the young lady and the older boy told me that it was his sister.

I went to the young lady and asked her if she was alright. She said that she had a really sharp pain in her stomach. I felt her head and she was burning up with fever. She began to shake all over. I asked the boys if there was an adult with them that could take her home. The older boy said that they had taken the bus into town but he was trying to call his father.

One of the workers from inside the restaurant where we were standing came out to see what the problem was. I told the lady that I needed cool towels and cold water so that I could cool down the girl's fever. When she returned with the cloths I asked her if I could bring the young lady into the restaurant so that she could get out of the hot sun.

As we went into the restaurant the boy returned and said that his father had told them to take the bus back home. I'm sure that the boy didn't tell his father how badly his sister was hurting. He probably just said that she didn't feel well, because I know that any parent would have been there if they had known the extent of her pain.

I wasn't about to send these children on the bus with her feeling the way she did, so I asked the boy if he would allow me to pay for a taxi to return them to their home. He said it would be okay, and I asked the lady in the restaurant to call a taxi for me.

While we were waiting I found out from this young girl that she had been feeling just fine a short time earlier and had just started feeling sick after eating some peanuts while on the bus. My first thought was that she was having an allergic reaction, which I knew could be extremely dangerous. I told her that as soon as she arrived home she needed to tell her father to take her to a doctor.

When the taxi arrived I asked the driver how much it would cost to take them to their home. He told me that it would cost $8.00. I gave him $20.00 and told him that I expected him to get them safely to their home and if she needed to stop along the way he needed to stop for her.

As I put them into the cab I told them to be safe and wished them God's blessings. As I turned to leave I realized that these young children were the reason that God had sent me to Long Beach. He gave me the opportunity to be their angel to get them safely home.

When I returned to the hotel I called Ben to tell him that God had sent me there for these young children, and I told him what had happened. I told him how good I felt about being able to be there for them, and the response I received from him was "You shouldn't have given the driver so much money, it could have been a scam!" I realized that he was never going to understand how satisfying it was to do something without expecting anything in return.

Each day I tried to find ways to reach out to others with the Love of Christ that was flowing through me. I learned that a simple smile could brighten up everyone's day. I enjoyed simply sharing my happiness with everyone.

I had coworkers approaching me each day telling me that they could tell that I was in the airport because they could hear me laughing all the way down the concourse. I was letting my light shine and I found that everyone wanted to be part of that light. God always gave me enough love to share!

Ben asked me several times to marry him, but I told him that I wasn't ready to be married again. I knew our relationship still needed some work before I could commit my life to him. We went to counseling because I knew we still had some issues that needed to be addressed. Ben wanted the counselor to tell me that I had built unrealistic walls around myself that I needed additional counseling to help to break down. He told the counselor that I had become too independent and needed to learn how to be more dependent on him.

What the counselor told us instead was that Ben had trust issues and anger from his childhood that he needed to deal with. The counselor told Ben that the cautions I had been taking were very healthy and necessary for my protection. Ben didn't like what we were told, so he shrugged it off and said that the counselor just took my side because she was a woman.

Ben had one son, but their relationship was not a very good one. Ben didn't approve of his son's wife and continued to tell him so. Ben also would tell him how he thought his son should be living his life. His son was tired of the constant criticism so he didn't have much contact with his father.

Ben tried to give me the space I needed to spend time with my children as the counselor suggested and things seemed to be getting better. After dating for three and a half years I agreed to marry him, believing that we could work out whatever problems still existed. I knew he would never be physically abusive to me, and I thought that I could deal with his emotional insecurities better if I was married to him. I hoped that by living in the same house he would not feel the need to pressure me to be with him more.

I also hoped that by marrying Ben it would free me from his financial debt and I wouldn't have to keep hearing him tell me that I didn't appreciate all he had done for me.

We planned the wedding for April, but in February of 2002 the house we were going to live in (Ben's house) burned to the ground. It was devastating for Ben, but I have to say on my life's Richter scale it was simply a 1.0 quake.

I had moved some of my items into the house and lost all my family photos and some precious items that I had received from my mom, but having left behind everything once before, I had realized that things are only things and you don't need them to be happy. This was the second time now that God reinforced to me that the people in my life are more important that any material object.

I tried to explain this to Ben, but he believed that his things made him who he was. Coming from an abusive childhood where he had nothing, he couldn't understand that the things he had were only superficial items. He believed that everything he owned showed the world that he was a great man. He said that he had struggled to build the successful life he was living and he hadn't needed anyone's help to get there. Ben felt the need to hold onto everything as if his life depended on them.

I married Ben in April at the home of Rachell and Artie. It was a small wedding with family and a few friends. As I prepared to walk down the stairs to the ceremony I told Libby that I didn't want to get married. She said that I didn't have to go through with it, but I told her that I felt like I owed it to Ben to give him a chance.

Even though I was moving farther away from all my children, I was determined to make time to see them and get to know my grandchildren.

We rebuilt the house while living in a fifth-wheel trailer on the property. I drew up the floor plan for the house, and it was going to be beautiful. Ben had injured his foot while on one of his jobs and wasn't able to drive his truck, so he decided to spend his time working as the general contractor in the building of our home.

A few months later Libby found out that she was pregnant with her first child, my third grandchild. She had some difficulties during this time, but we stood together as a family and rejoiced when she gave birth to her son.

Tanner was born six weeks early and was very small. He weighed only four pounds six ounces, but we could tell that he was a fighter. Libby had named him Tanner after my mom. Mom's maiden name was Tanner. After several weeks in the hospital he was able to come home. I was sure that Mom was watching over him while he was in the hospital. Tanner was so tiny, but his blue eyes showed us that he wasn't going to give up. He continued to thrive, and Libby was able to take him home from the hospital about two weeks after he was born.

During this time I had the opportunity to experience a marvelous event on one of my layovers in Chicago. I had gone into town with one of my coworkers, and after having dinner we walked out to Lake Michigan. As we approached the beach we could see a large group of people down the beach. It looked like they had built small sand castles all over the beach. I wanted to see what was going on so we went to find out. As we got closer we could see that what we thought were sand castles were actually brown paper bags set together in groups of four all over the beach.

There was a large banner hanging by them that said "BETWEEN FRIENDS." I asked one of the ladies standing in the group what they were doing and she told me that every October 1 they get together all over the nation to light candles for the victims of domestic violence. I got a huge lump in my throat and tears in my eyes as I told her that I had been a victim for eighteen years. She asked me if we would like to help them light the candles, and I felt honored to join them with this incredible act of caring. I called each of my children and told them that I was lighting a candle for each one of us. As I stood there and watched these candles glow I gave thanks again to God for saving me from the horrible life I had once lived. And I prayed for every soul that was now in a similar situation. I know that my being there that night was not by coincidence. I believe that God sent me there so that I could remember how great his mercy had been for me.

Chapter Sixteen

Because Ben wasn't bringing in any income I needed to work more to pay the bills. While Ben was busy working on the details for the house the subject of my being gone for work didn't come up as often. I flew six days a week and had very little time to do anything else, but it was exciting to be with him when he started selecting all the flooring and fixtures for the new home. I was expected to help with all the interior painting because Ben didn't want to pay for a painter to do it.

I had drawn up the floor plans for the new home, and I was very excited to see how it would turn out. It took us six months to re-build the house, and it turned out to be even more beautiful than I had imagined. Even though the house wasn't completely finished we moved in and it was great to have a real home to live in again.

I now was in charge of doing all the necessary paperwork for the insurance company. I had to itemize everything that had been in the house and come up with a value for each item. The adjuster told me to itemize each room separately and give him the list. The items would be paid for as soon as they were replaced. During the process of replacing all these items we were assigned to another agent that wanted me to rewrite the list of items differently. With keeping all the receipts and paperwork done and still trying to work I became very frustrated.

It wasn't until the house was finished that the issue of my working came up with Ben again. The thing that was most confusing to me was that Ben wanted me to be home with him, but he didn't spend any time with me when I was there. It made him happy to simply have me on the same property. I would call him at the shop when dinner was ready and he would come up to the house whenever he finished what he was doing. I would wait for fifteen minutes and then start without him. Ben would then talk on the phone while he ate and then return to the shop until bedtime.

Ben would try to get me to come down to the shop and just sit in there while he worked. He didn't understand that with only one day off I still needed to maintain the house, do the laundry and prepare his meals. We were still replacing furnishings, and I was trying to get the home in order.

With all of the work necessary to make our home livable I had no time left for myself. If I did take a day to sit and read, which I loved to do, Ben would always find something that he thought I needed to do. He acted as if I was wasting time by reading because he could always find something that needed to be done. He believed in his mind that if there was anything needing to be done, you couldn't waist time doing nothing. When I finished decorating the house Ben decided that I needed to start helping out with yard work.

I usually enjoyed working with plants and spent a lot of time planting flowers and making my yards beautiful. However, I found that I started resenting the fact that it had become my responsibility. I wanted to do it by choice, not because I had been told I that I had to. Ben would bring home plants for me to plant

T. L. MESSNER

and then felt he needed to remind me each day that I was home that it was my responsibility to water them.

I have to admit that I did what I was told, but I became more angry each time that I did it. I knew that I should just tell Ben how I felt, but I realized that I wasn't as strong as I once thought I was. When I did try to talk to Ben he would remind me of all the things he was doing as if to compare who had more responsibilities. Somehow his list was always longer than mine, and he couldn't understand that I was frustrated and tired and just wanted time to do nothing.

I wanted to find a way to bring some joy back into our home and decided to start making cookies and sharing them with the neighbors. I hadn't met many of them because we all lived on five-acre or larger lots. Though Ben had lived there for eighteen years he didn't know very many of his neighbors. I remembered the times as children when neighbors knew each other and had fun visiting when they passed on the street. I wanted to find new friends and decided that the best place to start was close to home. I decided to reach out to see who would respond and found that many of the neighbors enjoyed the special treats. The family across the street started calling me the cookie lady, and it was fun to see everyone's faces light up when they saw me coming.

Ben even started having fun delivering the goodies to the families in our neighborhood. Because the new house had a very large kitchen I started inviting friends and family members over to make Christmas candy like my mom had done years ago. We had such a wonderful time and everyone left with a large dish of candy for themselves, Ben and I delivered even more plates to all the neighbors. They all started looking forward to their unexpected treats, and I was having fun again.

I became good friends with one of our neighbors and started

112

attending church with her whenever I could get a Sunday off, and I felt like I was finally fitting in to this new life.

I was still responsible for paying the household debts. Ben hadn't worked for seven months, and we were living off of what I brought in as well as the insurance money from the fire, but the money was going fast.

To the outside world it looked as though we were very prosperous, but we were deeply in debt.

Ben wouldn't put my name on anything he owned, and I had to get permission from him to even talk to any of the companies about the payments I was making. He felt the need to own everything himself.

When he did return to work he spent a lot of time on the job, but all the money he made went right back into his company. Ben had started his own company shortly after I met him because he had always wanted to be his own boss.

I had encouraged him to follow through with his dream of having his own company because I knew it would make him happy. I knew that it would take several years to get his company off the ground, but five years later everything he earned went right back to the company. Very little was being contributed to the household bills.

With me being responsible for the household bills and Ben's bookkeeper taking care of the business affairs, Ben was oblivious to what he was spending. He continued to spend as though he had an endless well of money. He would simply hand me the bills that needed to be paid and tell me that I needed to pay them. I tried so many times to tell him that we didn't have the money, but he wouldn't listen.

I repeatedly asked him to please contribute to the household fund so I didn't have to work as much, and then I could be home with him more. The answer I always got was "You don't appreciate everything the company does for us. You won't support me with my dream the way I supported you with yours."

I reminded him that my dream brought with it a paycheck, and that it was a good thing because without it we wouldn't be able to make it. After many frustrating conversations about the subject I finally told him that I didn't want to be responsible for the paying bills anymore. His response was "If you won't even pay the bills then why did I marry you?

I replied, "I don't know, why did you marry me?" Ben's answer was, because I wouldn't just live with him.

After that statement, Ben walked away and I realized that my role in this marriage was simply to be cook, housekeeper and financial aid. I realized that I had made a terrible mistake and should have listened to my heart before marrying him. I felt like I had tried my very best to make our home a happy place, but every time I took a step forward, I was pushed back down. The stress I was feeling was starting to make me depressed and angry.

After the horrible events of September 11 my son-in-law Artie lost his job. He and Rachell lost their home and had to move to another state for them to find work. After they moved I found out the Rachell was pregnant again. I flew to their home for the birth of my first granddaughter, Hailey. Ben told me that he was too busy to go with me.

Hailey was our beautiful little princess. She weighed six pounds four ounces, and she looked just like Rachell when she was born. Hailey's eyes were an incredible blue color, and she had a head full of dark hair. She had the same little button nose that Hayden had and was so sweet.

I had to return home to go to work so I didn't get to spend very much time with them, but I promised them that I would return as often as I could. Just seven months after Hailey's birth my daughter Libby gave birth to my second granddaughter, Bailey.

Libby and Rachell had decided that because they were twins they would give their first daughters rhyming names. Bailey looked just like Libby when she was born. She weighed seven pounds four ounces, and her hair had a light tint of red in it. When we laid the two babies together they looked just like their mothers when they were born.

I started calling Bailey "Miss B" because I told the girls I would have to call them B and H so they would know who I was talking to.

Our year for girls continued when three months after Hailey's birth, Rachell became pregnant again. Seven months after Bailey was born we welcomed Harlie into our family.

With blue eyes and not much hair she was the spitting image of her father, Artie. She weighed seven pounds four ounces and was named Harlie Grace after my grandmother. I called her "Grandma's Gracie." I wasn't able to spend much time with them this trip either, but I was going to make sure that I made it down to see them whenever I could.

Ben and I had been married for four years, and I was determined to make my marriage work this time. I tried selling homemade items for extra money and I cleaned houses for the neighbors. I worked as much as I could so that we would have the money we needed to survive. While having to do so many extra things I was gone from home even more.

I realized that I wasn't devoting the time to my children and grandchildren that I wanted to, and I invited them to our house every day that I didn't have to work. While all my family was there my house was full and I loved it. I always said that grandmas get to say yes even if everyone else says no. That's our right as grandmas!

It became very hurtful to me when Ben couldn't simply be a grandpa. He felt like he needed to constantly give the grandchildren the discipline that he didn't feel their parents were giving them. He was always after them to not eat with their fingers or not to talk with their mouth full. Ben had a very loud voice, and when he would talk to them I could see fear in their eyes. Our dinner table became a battlefield. Ben claimed that he was teaching them respect, but I saw it differently.

I just wanted the children to have fun at Grandma and Grandpa's house, and I know my children wanted the same thing. Ben also felt that he needed to give my children advice on how he believed they should be raising their children. He tried to give them advice about the other aspects of their lives as well. He would call them to make sure they were doing whatever it was that he had told them to do and would become angry if they didn't.

I told him that he could give them all the advice he wanted to but he couldn't make them take it, nor was he allowed to get angry if they didn't.

My children began to pull away from Ben and therefore me too. They started turning down my invitations to come for dinner because it was too hard for them to hear the constant criticism from Ben.

Ben came to me one day and told me that he didn't feel like I appreciated everything he had done for me. He told me that if I had helped him fix his teeth he would thank me every time he looked into the mirror. I asked him if that was what he expected from me, and he said that if I would do it he would feel more appreciated.

Once I realized the depth of admiration he expected from me I was determined to give him back every single cent he had ever spent on me. A short time later I received a settlement from an auto accident I had been in at work and I paid him back every bit of his money he had ever spent on me and told him that I was now free from his emotional and financial debt for good.

Ben then convinced all his friends that I didn't love him as much as I loved my job. He made them feel sorry for him and they started bringing dinner to the house or inviting him out for dinner while I was working.

He would call me to tell me that someone was taking him out so that I would feel guilty for not being there with him. Having a job that required me to be gone for days at a time was hard enough without being made to feel guilty for it.

Ben had become negative about everything. I think he could tell that I was drifting away. I didn't want to call home when I got to my layovers because I had been so happy at work and all I would hear from Ben when I called was negativity. He would complain about who said they would call and didn't or how someone had screwed him over at work, or even worse, who wasn't grateful enough for something he had done for them.

I felt like I had become just a person to complain to. He never asked how my day had been or how I was doing. He just wanted me to share in his sorrows.

After four and a half years of marriage I realized that this wasn't where I wanted to spend the rest of my life. I couldn't make things better, and by now I didn't want to try anymore. It felt like all my efforts to make things work were being wasted. I decided that if I was going to struggle to pay bills they should be my own bills and not those placed upon me.

On the day that I finally told Ben that I was done and I was leaving he acted like my decision had come completely by surprise. Even though we had gone to counseling two times during our marriage he thought that I would look past all the problems.

Ben thought that if he ignored the problems long enough they would just go away. After spending eight years with him his problems were indeed going away… I was leaving.

We talked for several hours about why I couldn't stay in the marriage any longer, and I never even cried. I think I was so ready for it to be over that it made leaving easier. The only thing Ben remembered from the conversation was that I had told him that I really hadn't wanted to get married again. I told him that I married him because I felt like I owed it to him to try.

I felt like I needed to repay my debt to him. I felt that I had tried my very best to be the wife he needed me to be, but I couldn't try any more. I told him that making me solely responsible for his happiness was not fair to me. He needed to find a way to be happy himself. I also told Ben that there is someone out there that can be all the things he needs a wife to be, but that person isn't me. I had tried my best to make him happy and instead made myself unhappy. I told him that the things he needed in a wife were not the things that I was able to give him. I couldn't put aside my children and grandchildren and pretend that I didn't love my job just so he could feel better.

When Ben's friends asked him what had happened all he could think to tell them was that I never wanted to marry him to begin with. That was the only reason he could come up that didn't put any blame on him, so again everything became my fault.

It didn't matter to me what his friends thought, because I knew the people who knew me would know the truth and I didn't care what the others thought. I told Ben that I would take only the things that were mine before the marriage, and I told him that I knew he could find the woman he was meant to be with. I just hoped that Ben had learned enough from our problems to be able to be a better husband for the next woman in his life.

Chapter Seventeen

Ben called my daughter Libby after I left and asked her if she thought I was really done as I had said. He wanted to know if there was something he could do to convince me to come back. Libby surprised me with the insight of her answer to him. She told him that for men, when they say that they are done they will come back after three days and say that they want to try again. However, for a woman to get to the point of saying that she is done she will have already tried everything within her power to make things work. Without having success, she will come to the conclusion that she is done. Libby assured him that I truly was done!

Ben made sure that the divorce was taken care of very quickly because he was afraid that I would try to take his precious things away from him. I never even attempted to take his things. I took only the personal items that were mine before our marriage and a few pieces of furniture we bought after the fire. There were a great many precious items we had acquired during our marriage that I would have loved to have, but I didn't want the negativity of fighting for them.

Anyone entering our home would not have been able to tell that I had taken anything at all. I didn't even fight for my share of the value of the house and five acres that it was built on. I didn't want to spend years fighting, even though I was the one that struggled to make the house payments. I knew that Ben would fight with all his strength to hold onto what he considered precious…his things!

I already had everything that was precious to me, and they weren't things. I had my children and grandchildren and the knowledge that God would provide me with whatever I was in need of.

I left Ben in November right before Thanksgiving and was able to stay with Libby and her family while I looked for a place to live.

I had already booked and paid for a cruise that Christmas for Ben and myself. Rachell and Artie were going to go also, but Artie had broken his leg earlier and wasn't able to join us. I decided that because I couldn't get back any of the money I had paid for the tickets, I was still going to go with Rachell.

Rachell and I had the most wonderful time! We went to the Western Caribbean, where we explored Grand Caymans, Cozumel, and Ocho Rios. We made great memories and laughed and danced and just had a wonderful time being together. We climbed a waterfall in Ocho Rios and explored the city of Grand Cayman and toured Cozumel.

After returning from our cruise I immediately went on the hunt for an apartment to live in. I found a small apartment to live in and again my home was filled with love and peace. I had to start from scratch to supply my apartment with all the necessary items, but I knew that it didn't matter if they were new or not because they were just things. And even though my kitchen was now extremely small I started making cookies for all my neighbors again. I got some very strange looks from the neighbors but I enjoyed reaching out to them with love.

I also made holiday aprons for the flight attendants that I flew with on the holidays and gave away many to passengers that found joy in my aprons. I had found that I receive a great deal of joy from giving to others with no expectation of getting anything in return. The smiles I created were more payment than any other reward I could ask for.

I know that the kindnesses I share with others each day are being shared with others down the line. It takes so little to start the ball of love rolling!

Shortly after returning from the cruise I decided that I was going to take advantage of the benefits of my job. I wanted to start seeing the world; after all, that was one of the reasons why I wanted to be a flight attendant.

I had always wanted to see castles, and I wanted to go to Germany to see them. I called my close friends from flight attendant training, MaryAnn and Joann, and told them that I was going. I told them that if they wanted to join me I would love to have their company, but if not I would go alone. Both MaryAnn and Joann said that they wanted to go with me, and we started making plans.

We decided to go not only to Germany but also Austria and Italy. For two weeks we traveled through the countries and enjoyed the beauties of this world that God created for us. I was living in Heaven!

We started in Germany, where I did indeed get to see castles, and then went to Salzburg, Austria, where we went on the Sound of Music tour. After Austria we went to Venice, where we had a room that was right on the canal. We spent two days walking through the streets of Venice, where I was on the hunt for a wedding cake topper for Libby's wedding that was planned for the next July. I finally found the perfect topper. It was a Venetian blown glass statue of a couple dancing. I carried it around for the next week just praying that I could get it home without breaking it. While we were walking through Venice we ran across a Messner Hotel. It was exciting to see my name on a sign; even though our family name was German, it was fun to see it in Italy.

We then went to Rome, where we explored the Coliseum and other ruins. We were also able to see the Vatican. We went from Rome to La Spezia and walked through the cliff cities of Cinque Terre. We had packed warm clothes because the forecasts had showed that it would be rainy, but every day was beautiful and around eighty degrees. I started telling Maryann and Joann that it was because I was so happy that the sun followed me everywhere I went.

I even mastered the video camera and drove MaryAnn and Joann crazy filming our adventures. We recorded some wonderful memories on the tapes and can watch them now and have fun all over again. I felt like I had finally found the happiness that I had searched so diligently for throughout my whole life It surprised me to see how easy it was to be happy. All I had to do was wake up each day with the determination to bring happiness to everyone else that crossed my path throughout the day.

I was now starting each day with a prayer to God asking him to lead me to the people that needed me. And I prayed that He would guide me as to what I would need to say or do. I wanted to be God's hands on earth and reach out to His children and help them return to Him. I prayed that God's light would shine through me and that I could make each person that crossed my path a little happier than they were before.

Chapter Eighteen

Libby is now married to a great man, Lee, and they have two beautiful children, Tanner and Bailey. They continue to show me how a real family is supposed to be, filled with love and kindness. They have constant love and appreciation for each other, and I know that both Tanner and Bailey will grow up knowing how loved they are by both their parents.

Libby has a tender heart that feels the true emotion of other people's feelings and works very hard to never crush the spirit of those she loves. I see so much of me in her. I have watched her learn things the hard way (as I did) but also become strong by enduring those things with strength. One of my greatest compliments came from Libby when she told me, "The thing I love about you most is that no matter how bad I screw up, I know you will always love me." More than anything else, this is the one thing I want my family to know without a doubt. That I truly will love them no matter what happens.

Rachell and Artie are still holding onto each other and have three beautiful children, Hayden, Hailey and Harlie. Their road has been rough, but they are determined to keep their family together. Rachell is working in the medical field and is very happy helping others. Hayden, Hailey and Harlie are very blessed to have parents that will continue to teach them about love and the importance of working as a family.

Rachell is my social butterfly. She loves to be with people and brings joy to everyone. She has my free spirit and wants to experience everything life has to offer. She is quick to laugh (even when you have done something totally stupid) and she's just as quick to bring comfort when it's needed. If she sees you fall she will make sure you are alright before she breaks up laughing. I say this with love because we have all found great fun in this.

Scott is a single father at this time, but he is a wonderful dad. He enjoys riding stunted street bikes and is really great at it. It still scares me to watch him because I don't want him to get hurt, but he has mastered all the necessary techniques and can perform with the best. Scott's son Rylan is also learning to ride dirt bikes and is following in the steps of his father. Rylan is blessed to have a compassionate and loving father to show him the correct way to love and respect the women in his life.

Scott has worked hard and has gone from being a delivery driver to a management position where he is respected and liked by all the employees he works with. He has continued to be a loving man I can be proud of.

Scott is my entertainer "the rapper." He has more compassion in his heart than he can see. Like me Scott is a dreamer. There are things he longs to do in his life but hasn't yet been able to live those dreams. I know that someday he will! He also is not a quitter, and I know someday he will accomplish everything he sets his mind to. The respect he has shown to me and his sisters is truly a testimony to his loving heart.

In spite of the examples he had in his life, he is able to be a better man that those around him. He understands that actions can break or heal hearts.

We are still the "Four Musketeers." We have seen each other through heartaches and also rejoiced in each other's accomplishments. The bond we have shared is something that others will never understand. We are our own island of security in a world that has tried to destroy us. We know that whatever we may be faced with, we can always turn to each other for strength and guidance. We are never alone!

I am now planning our first ever sisters trip with Penny, Sheri and Peggy. We are going to spend a week on the island of Kauai, and for the first time in years we will be getting together for something other than a funeral. I am hoping that we can find a special sisterhood that will hold us all together for the rest of our lives.

Even though my life is wonderful now, I can't say that it is always easy. I still struggle daily, but I know that with God's help I can overcome any struggles I may face. I don't spend time wondering where the money will come from because I trust that God would provide for me everything I will need.

Each day is an adventure that I will gladly explore!

After three divorces you would think that I would give up entirely on men, but I do believe that God wants me to have a healthy relationship with someone that will love me for who I am.

Another of my dear friends told me that I look at the world through rose-colored glasses and that I need someone to watch out for me. She was very concerned when I started dating again even though it had been a year since my divorce; she thought it was too soon.

I told her that I like living in my rose-colored world. I don't want to look at every person and try to find things about them that might hurt me. I want to look for the good in everyone. I also told her that I'm not afraid of getting hurt again because I know I will be alright. I have learned how to pick myself up and carry on.

This dance has been mastered!

After being encouraged by some coworkers to join Match.com I met David. His profile first caught my attention because his opening line said "Oh Miss Are You For Me?" I wrote to him and told him that I must be the one he was looking for because I get called "Oh Miss" about a thousand times a day.

As soon as we met we were instantly attracted to each other. We had so much fun and laughed the whole night. We are still together and the fun still continues. David loves me just the way I am. He never even asked about my past and is just learning about it all through this book. And YES he still loves me!

He understands like me, that it doesn't matter how you got to where you are now. What matters is who you become in the end.

We have traveled to many places together and have enjoyed a relationship that is easy. I didn't think I would ever be able to say that a relationship was easy, but we have mutual respect and appreciation for each other.

I can't say that I wish that I had met David before all the other bad relationships, because I believe that I wouldn't have been the same person I am now. If I had met him earlier I may not have been able to appreciate him for the wonderful man he is.

I can finally say that "I LIKE WHO I AM!" That is the most powerful statement in my life!

After many years of dying my hair blonde and straightening it with chemicals I have gone natural again. I am learning to appreciate my naturally curly red hair (gray and all)!

I now laugh with all my heart and love with all my strength!

I am still living my dream of flying, and I continue to bake and share with my neighbors the joys that God has given me. God has now directed me to tell my story to the world in hopes of allowing others in pain to see that they don't need to remain in their pain for the rest of their lives.

This book was inspired by a dream I had one night. In this dream I was holding a book. the title of the book was *Three Women and the Men They Dance With*.

After telling David about this dream he told me to write down the title because it was either a book I was supposed to read or possibly I was to write it. Either way I should write down the title and I would find out its meaning later. I went on the hunt for this book, but was unable to find it anywhere. I knew that I was not a writer, so I put the thoughts of the book aside and forgot about it.

A few months later I was working with a great woman, Julia. We started talking about dreams, and I told her of this book from my dream. I told her that I didn't understand the meaning because I couldn't find this book anywhere. Julia told me that the way I relayed my life experiences I could be a great writer. Still not believing myself to have anything worth writing about, I thanked her for her confidence in me and headed home. The title was stuck in my head as I drove home, but I couldn't imagine what I could write about that would be of interest to anyone else. Then I received the inspiration I was looking for. I realized that I have been three very different women throughout my lifetime.

Because of situations I have found myself in I was totally different in each phase of my learning. I have told my story to many people over the years and have had many of them tell me that they have been inspired by my experiences. So I realized that I was supposed to write this book and it needed to be about me. I went home and started telling my story again, this time on paper.

I know that God wants me to share my trials and mistakes as well as my joys in overcoming them with the world. And I believe that there are a lot of people in this crazy world that can find comfort in knowing that they are not alone in their pain.

I have found that by sharing my story with others it has given them a feeling of comfort and they want to open up and share with me painful things that they have kept hidden from the world. I am grateful that I have been chosen by God to reach out to these hurting souls to help them learn to let go of the anger and hurt they are holding inside.

The woman I am now has been created by the dances I had to learn along my journey. I hope someday I can share all the wonderful places I have seen with my children and grandchildren.

I am telling my story not in hopes of gaining sympathy, but instead, of showing how my life has been changed forever by having experienced these events. If my experiences and struggles can inspire even one hurting soul to find comfort in the arms of our God and Savior Jesus Christ, then all my trials and tears have not been in vain!!

Chapter Nineteen

I believe that each one of us has a purpose in this life, and finding out what that purpose is will bring you great joy and peace! It is different for each one of us, but I know that my purpose is to bring joy to everyone God sends through my life's journey, even if it's just through a smile in passing. That is why I smile and say hello to everyone.

It is great to watch the reactions of strangers. Some will totally ignore you while others will look at you as if to say "do I know you?" And some will truly light up and say "Hello" in return.

I believe that each one of us wants to be noticed, even if it is by a stranger for only one moment. We need to know that someone acknowledges that we are in this world.

I know that through my travels God has placed people in my path for the purpose of uplifting them and helping them along their journey. I may never realize the depth of the impact God has made in their lives with my help.

I have also been blessed on occasion to see the results of His great work right away. I am grateful to be able to recognize God's hand in every step I take through these dances I am doing now. I will continue to be God's hands on this Earth, knowing that he will guide me through any dances I may still need to learn.

The life's dances to where I am now have not been easy ones. Through choices of my own and choices made by others in my life, I have struggled to learn how to be strong emotionally and spiritually.

The trials and hardships put in my way were not things that I wanted to learn, but rather the things that God needed me to learn!

I read a statement after my second divorce which has a statement that has become my motto for life. It states:

I AM A SURVIVOR OF PHYSICAL AND EMOTIONAL ABUSE. I NO LONGER VIEW MYSELF AS A VICTIM. THE CHANGE HAS COME FROM INSIDE ME… MY ATTITUDE. I DO NOT NEED TO DESTROY MYSELF WITH ANGER AND HATE. I DON'T NEED TO ENTERTAIN THOUGHTS OF REVENGE.

MY SAVIOR KNOWS WHAT HAPPENED. HE KNOWS THE TRUTH. HE WILL MAKE THE JUDGEMENTS AND THE PUNISHMENTS. HE WILL BE JUST!

I WILL LEAVE IT IN HIS HANDS.

I WILL NOT BE JUDGED FOR WHAT HAPPENED TO ME, BUT I WILL BE JUDGED FOR HOW I LET IT AFFECT MY LIFE!

I AM RESPONSIBLE FOR MY ACTIONS AND WHAT I DO WITH MY KNOWLEDGE!

It would be easy for me to hold a grudge or be angry at life, but I choose to let these trials make me a better person.

Modern medicine now even states that harboring strong emotions such as hate and resentment can enhance disease in an existing condition or even cause one to start!

The trials and hurts of life can't be avoided, so I choose to dance through them and rejoice in the great joys of my life!

These three women have made me the woman I am today! Because my life is not yet finished, I don't know how many more changes this woman will be in store for, or if with the passing years age will create a new woman. I do know, however, that she will be strong and focused on the adventures yet to come!

I know that I am in the arms of my Savior and I will trust Him to show me the way!

He knows all the steps to every dance, and He will always lead me in the right direction!

AFTER ALL…LIFE TRULY IS A DANCE!!

CPSIA information can be obtained at www.ICGtesting.com
Printed in the USA
BVOW01s1015170614

356536BV00001B/2/P